Boomers: Visions of the *New* Retirement

Boomers: Visions of the *New* Retirement

Dr. Maria K. Malayter

iUniverse, Inc.

New York Lincoln Shanghai

Boomers: Visions of the *New* Retirement

iUniverse, Inc.

For information address:
iUniverse, Inc.
2021 Pine Lake Road, Suite 100
Lincoln, NE 68512
www.iuniverse.com

ISBN: 0-595-31506-2

This book is dedicated to the late Helena Julia Malayter O'Brien. It was her courage and character that inspired this book and to always pursue my dreams. Your sense of service and spirituality caused transformation in my own life. I appreciate the contribution you have been throughout my life. Thank you so much Aunt Helen! I love you and miss you dearly!

Contents

Acknowledgements

I acknowledge the following people for the love and support I received through the process of writing this book. Thank for believing in me!

God: the inspiration behind this project.

My parents. Thank you for the gift of life It is through your loss that I have strength.

My grandparents. Though in my life a short time your love helped me survive the loss of my parents. Thanks for teaching me to be good in school!

My Aunt Helen for listening to me talk about all the theorists and believing I can achieve whatever I want. Thanks for being a model of strength.

My brothers, Matt and Fred. Thanks for asking hard questions and supporting me. Thanks for teaching me to stand up for myself. Matt, thanks for sending me funny mashed potato photos and encouraging notes.

Anna, my new mom and Dawn, my new sister, Thanks for believing in me.

The Sassy Sisters, Kristen, Amy, Lisa and Dawn. I appreciate your listening to me throughout this project and for having fun events to let my hair down.

Sue New who listened all the way through!

Amy Pauszek for always having an open ear as I have been working through this project. I have appreciated the encouragement.

Sharon Qualls for always coaching me through, helping me make a plan, and holding me to my commitments.

Jason and Lisa Starzec...for feeding me throughout the entire process. I would have starved. Thanks for listening to me during the tough times.

Voula Popovich for helping with editing along the way!

James Kelher for assisting with graphics during the process.

Ann Campanella for encouraging me to "get published".

Bill Owen for supporting and cheering me on!

Travis Wynberry, for listening and being supportive. Thanks for the technology support and encouragement during the process.

Matt Cira, for always being available to eat chicken and mashed potatoes at Johnny's.

Matt Galvin for always knowing I would finish my PhD and write a book!

My dissertation committee, Dr. Ruth Maurer, the late Professor Coblentz, and Dr. Stein, and Dr. Gary Gemmill and Dr. Bill Barkley. Thanks for the encouragement and commitment to move me to completion!

Dr. Marvel Lang, for being a mentor and source of strength throughout this process!

The technology team of Collegis at National-Louis University. Without your support, I would have never been able to complete this book! I want to give special thanks to Ester Barazza and Greg Grunewald for staying late to fix my computer before I had to leave for summer school at Indiana University; Travis Wynberry for designing a conceptual framework in Powerpoint, helping me find software to complete the program and for making sure I was taken care of always. Matt Cira for saving all my files before the laptop crashed. James Kelher for always asking, "When is your defense?", fixing my tables for my appendix, and lots of other computer help. Ron Morvay, Kevin Hickey, Greg Grunewald, and John Mazariegos for helping me fix all different types of things on my computer.

Marlene Brown, who supported my own healing and sharing the power of Reiki!

Martha Casazza and Stephen Thompson for their support and encouragement.

My friends at Mailboxes, Etc., Tim, Jim, Damian, Tim Jr. and Tiffany, for mailing and printing all of my materials throughout my entire degree process.

My life coaches, Rami Henrich and Marilyn Varn. Thanks for holding me up and coaching me to make it!

Jeff Polnau, who always was asked to be remembered in anything I published.

My former employees, students, and friends that helped create the idea for this project. Your impact was so large.

My interview participants: your contribution may help so many people.

Again, I dedicate this work to God. For He carried me when I was shattered and blinded in this process. Thank you for the love and light that surrounds my life. I am truly blessed!

Introduction

The story begins in August 1993 at the Great Lakes Naval Training Center. I was in my mid-twenties and starting a new position with the Pacific Institute for Research and Evaluation. I was the director of the PREVENT (Personal Responsibility Values Education and Training) program, a health lifestyles training program designed to increase personal and professional readiness for military personnel, at the Great Lakes, Illinois site. I was hired to increase enrollment and utilization of the program. This role led to my first facilitator recruitment where I made my initial acquaintance with a military retiree. He was a retired Air Force colonel and was interested in making a contribution through teaching and training. In my over ten year friendship with the retired colonel, I learned about the transition in retirement.

In addition to working with the U. S. Navy at Great Lakes, I taught as an adjunct professor for several of the local colleges and universities. Much to my surprise, many retirees appeared in my classroom to pursue further education or to change careers. I kept in contact with many of these retirees to track their experience in retirement. We have continued to have great friendships. I mentored them in the transition into retirement and they mentored me in my career. When I became a full time professor at National-Louis University in Applied Behavioral Science, I had the opportunity to offer many of my retiree friends the opportunity to teach at the college level and pass on their wealth of knowledge. The retirees' students received many benefits from the life experiences presented in class and the retirees loved contributing to tomorrow's future.

In my experiences, I learned retirees were everywhere in my professional life wanting to contribute to the future generations and to pursue intellectual endeavors. Within the seven years of my work with the U.S. Navy, I met many individuals preparing for retirement and then reinventing their lives in retirement. This led me to conduct academic research on the personal and professional experience and transition into retirement.

My academic research has been timely with the upcoming Baby Boomer retirement. The Baby Boomer generation is approaching retirement age and society will be surprised if preparation is not considered. This book addresses many of the issues of the transition into retirement and the impact of increased retirees in society. Some Boomers are already entering retirement or retiring early and the Boomer retirements will greatly increase within the next decade. How will we as a society respond?

The book is organized in three sections: defining retirement, the personal and organizational experience of retirement and the New Retirement. It is based upon my research conducted throughout my professional and academic career. Specifically, it has been the foundation for my doctoral dissertation. The book is written in an academic manner but still maintains much valuable information for the Boomer heading toward retirement and the human resource professional in succession planning as we experience the Great Boomer retirement.

The concepts that follow will inspire you to consider your own retirement and to explore the New Retirement. It my hope this book comes to you as a sign of hope for your future in your retirement and assists you in your transition. Are you ready for the truth about retirement? I invite you to turn the next page to begin your journey.

Section 1:
Defining Retirement

1

Background and History of Retirement

To further understand what has shaped retirement, it is important to review the origins of retirement, which was originally a time for rest and relaxation. The intent of retirement pay was to assist the person in the last years of life. The origination of retirement pay links from a combination of workers at age 64 toiling at the workplace and the pension system created for the Union army of disabled veterans from the Civil War (Costa, 1998). The pensions for veterans initiated the creation of a system to provide financial assistance to individuals unable to work due to old age and disability and to allow the individual some rest time before dying. Another contributor to the development of retirement pay was the implementation of private pensions, initiated by American Express in 1875. "It provided benefits for employees 60 years of age or over who had 20 years service with the company and were incapacitated for further performance of duty" (Social Security Administration, 2002a). Retirement, as a part of the lifecycle, was not recognized through benefit programs. Additional public policies were soon to follow.

Sixty-five as a mandatory retirement age was implemented with the formulation of Social Security by the Commission on Economic Security in 1934 (DeWitt, 1999). In 1935, Social Security included three programs of assistance, in collaboration with state governments: Old Age Insurance, Old Age and Survivors Insurance and Old Age Assistance (DeWitt, 1999). With 65 the age of retirement to receive Social Security benefits, the demarcation line of old age was created. The Committee on Economic Security selected the age 65 based on four factors (a) the existing private pensions using the age 65, (b) the state pension systems with half using 65 and the other half using 70, (c) the federal Railroad Retirement System, using the age 65, passed by Congress in 1934, and (d) the actuarial studies conducted by the Committee on Economic Security planners. (Social

Security Administration, 2002c). This was when life expectancy was estimated close to the age of 70. Mandatory retirement policies were created to protect the rights of the employee to earn the reward of retirement pay. With the onset of the creation of retirement policies and an increase of individuals entering retirement, the role and activities of a retired person began to develop.

The initial policies of retirement focused upon the financial assistance offered to retiring individuals. However, other aspects of coverage in retirement originated from the early implementations of health and other insurance covering service members through the War Risk Insurance Act of 1917 (Corning, 1969). Again, the systems and policies for retirement evolved out of benefits offered to military service members. In the evolution of the War Risk Insurance Act and expansion of group health insurance, the military enacted a "medicare" program to provide government health insurance for armed forces dependents (Corning, 1969). The model led to the creation of the nationwide program of Medicare, health insurance for the aged, under the Social Security amendments passed by Congress in 1965. The combination of financial assistance, health insurance, and private pensions for the aged allowed the model of retirement benefits to unfold. President Johnson also created the Older Americans Act and established the Administration on Aging to place a focus upon aging studies in America (SSA, 2002a). Retirement benefits became a human resource department initiative for organizations through the financial regulations and government benefit requirements.

Retirement is still viewed as a reward for a long-term commitment to a career, but there has been a shift from mandatory retirement to voluntary retirement. The evolution of voluntary retirement occurred when individual private pensions allowed the early access to early retirement through financial strategies and early access to financial accumulations. Voluntary retirement was also influenced by the governmental early retirement option at 62 in 1977 (DeWitt, 1999). Although Social Security benefits are reduced by electing to retire at 62, the loss in financial rewards can be made up through private pensions. With planning, the individual can be empowered to make the decision to retire early.

Another early retirement incentive was enacted through the Military Retirement Reform Act of 1986, Redux, where at 20 years of service the retiree received 40% of basic pay compared to at 30 years of service he or she received 75% (Smith, 2001). The policy was designed to encourage a higher retention rate within the organization. However, the situation had a reverse effect allowing more service members to retire early and prepare for second careers in the civilian sector. The situation created a training initiative for transition into the civilian world versus a retirement planning course. The transition assistance program was developed to assist the early retirees to adjust and prepare for life in the civilian sector.

Recently,

> Congress passed legislation to improve retirement benefits under Redux. Under the legislation, service members covered under Redux can choose either a one-time $30,000 bonus or better retirement benefits. If they choose the bonus, they would keep the current Redux benefits but receive the lump sum bonus at the 15-year mark in return for agreeing to serve at least 20 years.(Smith, 2001, p. 307)

Again, the military shift in career length modeled the incentive to retire early and impacted the original models of retirement pay and career length. The program devised by the government became a model for many other organizations to downsize organizations.

In business strategy, early retirement is an incentive system often used by an organization for restructuring. Early retirement is a reward for the employee and a benefit to the organization. Voluntary retirement allows the organization to offer early retirement incentives to lower the bottom line costs by allowing seasoned employees to choose to retire early with special benefit packages. The more seasoned employee costs much more than a younger employee. Further, early retirement incentives have also evolved as a strategy to reorganize and downsize the workforce, which has also allowed younger workers to move up the organization.

Numbers of those retiring early are on the rise (Sunoo, 1997), and the United States is experiencing much greater longevity with some individuals living into the 100's (Lach, 1999; Wagner, 1999). The shift in longevity is impacting the original concepts of retirement. Participation in early retirement of men aged fifty-five to sixty-four has increased; combined with an increase of life expectancy could lead to additional year that will be spent in retirement (Costa, 1998; Lee 1996). Today, the roles and activities of a retired person are different from the early days of Social Security. The expectations of persons above the age of 50 are shifting partially due to the increase in longevity. With this shift, all patterns of the life course are challenged. To conclude, the experience of retirement in a lifetime is challenged, and further understanding of retirement pay, benefits, and activities is necessary for organizational success.

2

The Problem with the Boomers' Retirement

This study investigated the shift occurring within the model of retirement, specifically in the area of preretirement training. Human resource professionals have had a responsibility to work with employees as they plan their retirement. However, it is unclear if this planning has been sufficient for early retirees. Thus, this study explored the experience and needs of early retirees in retirement in order to assist human resource professionals' organizational planning for preretirement training. The study examined the increasing trend of early retirement and the support provided to the early retirees from human resource departments. The early retiree, in this study, was someone who had left a career job before the age of 65 and was receiving money follow the departure from this job. Transition, understanding, preretirement training, decision-making, and relatedness are terms that shaped the study. Retirement was defined in this study as departure from career job and receiving money from a source following the departure.

Human resource departments continue to react and plan based upon the notion that retiring individuals finish work and head into rest and relaxation (Sunoo, 1997). The human resource departments of many organizations are not basing preretirement training on the employees' needs but are driven by compliance to government policy and cost effectiveness for the organization (Duleboh, Ferris, & Stodd, 1995). The preretirement training and planning encompasses the adherence to public policies requiring organizations to offer health benefits and pensions after retirement (Sullivan, 1992). Therefore, the focus of human resource departments for retirees is upon the health benefit planning and financial planning for retirement. Human resource departments are challenged with the organizational commitments of a work-life balance and the government regulations when preparing employees for retirement.

The concept of retirement is multifaceted, as demonstrated in the concept map presented as Figure 1. One aspect of retirement that could be explored is the individual's identity development in retirement. Another aspect of retirement could explore the planning and decision making for retirement both before and after the actual retirement event. Further, the study of retirement could focus on the impact on an organization when employees retire. Along with the focus on organizations, the human resource professional role with retirees could be explored for the purpose of preparation and planning to assist the retiring employee. Finally, the retirement stereotypes and actual activities could be studied to understand the actual experience of retirees. Each segment of the concept map presents a different area of potential study.

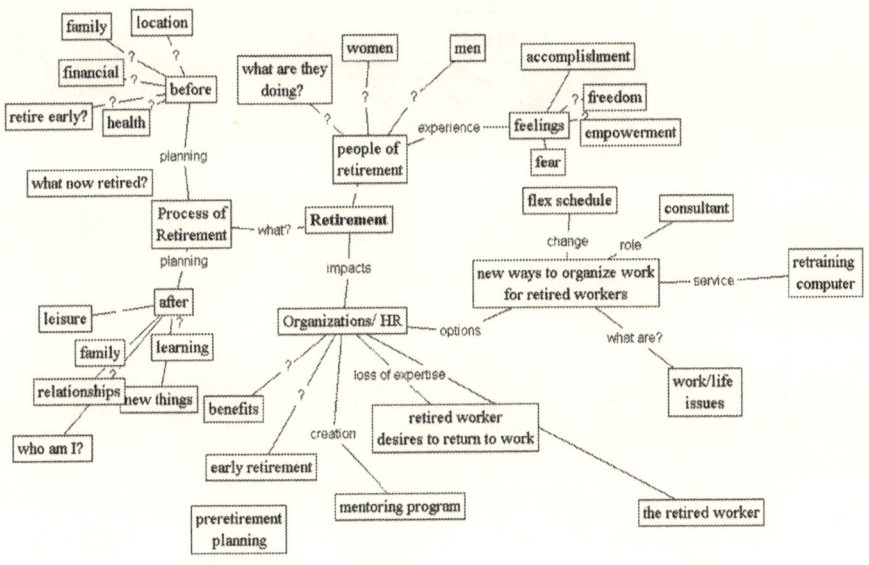

Figure 1. Retirement concept map.

The broad scope of potential research topics on the subject of retirement is much greater than what was accomplished within this study. Therefore, the scope of this study was limited to a focus on the application of the preretirement training provided by the human resource department to the early retiree and the resulting satisfaction for that retiree. Figure 2 focuses on the concept map section related to planning before retirement. In the concept map below, the following life issues and questions were explored to gain more information about retirement preparation and planning.

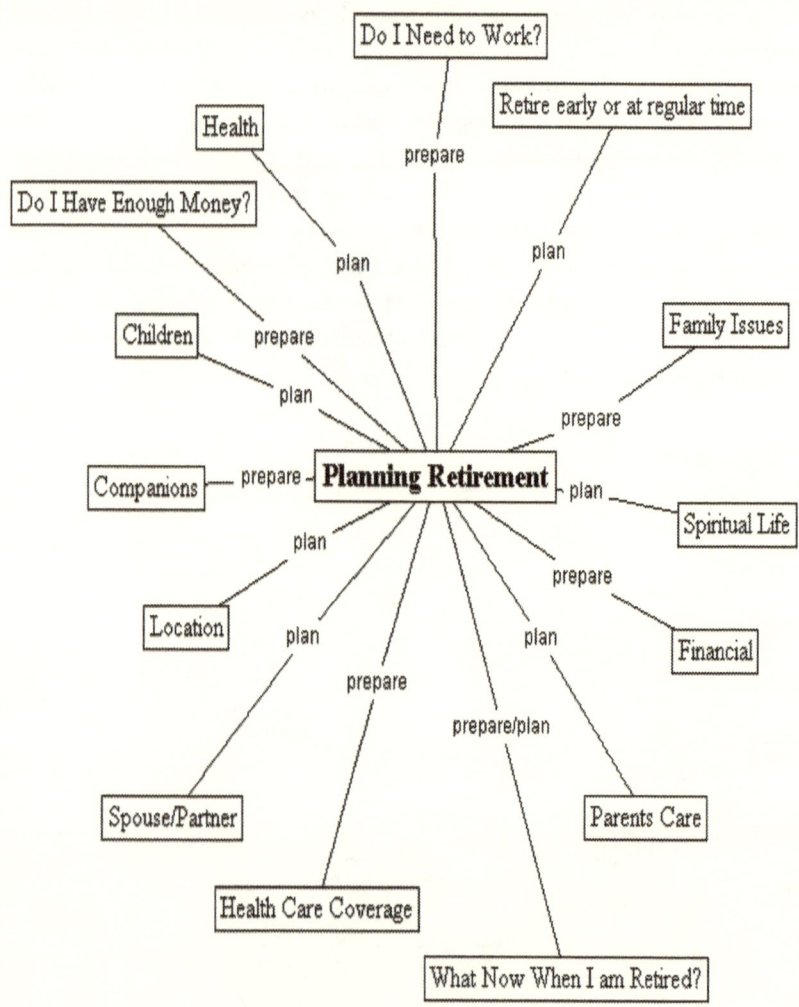

Figure 2. Planning for retirement map.

With the current re-engineering and consolidation of businesses, many companies are offering early retirement to some employees as an incentive to lower
their overall budgets by releasing the higher paid, longer tenured employee.
Thus, society is experiencing a larger population of retirees compared to earlier
generations (Gendell, 2001; Gowan, 1998). The increase in retirees is a combination of population growth and more organizations offering early retirement
incentives. As the average life span is increasing and the baby boomer generation

nears early and traditional retirement ages, the population of retirees will increase.

The baby boomer generation will effect retirement in many areas of society, including an increase in early retirement. Poulous (1997) clarified many traits and policy issues that will impact the retirement of the baby boomers.

On average the post-World War II baby boom generation has done better in terms of education, income and wealth than any prior generation in history. There has traditionally been strong public policy support in the U.S. for allowing maximum individual choice in decisions related to retirement and working. While many older persons have always worked well into their older years, the clear preference currently is for earlier retirement. Life expectancy is increasing, as is "healthy" life expectancy.

> The structure of work has changed and continues to change dramatically in the post-industrial era. (Poulos, 1997, pp. 54–55)

The alarming fact of an increase of retirees in the population presents the problem of the fiscal inability of the system of Social Security to support the many baby boomers heading toward retirement in 2010 (Steinbrink & Cook, 2002). The number of beneficiaries needing coverage in the system will outweigh the amount of money available in the system. Old Age and Survivors Insurance and Disability Insurance will be depleted in 2029 and Medicare between 2001 and 2005 (Costa, 1989). More recent studies predict the cash deficit for Social Security as early as the years 2016 to 2030 (Steinbrink & Cook, 2002) with the projected depletion date about the year 2038 (Williamson, 2002). The projections have been updated to reflect the following data from the Social Security Administration.

> The OASDI trust funds are projected to begin paying out more in benefits and other costs than they collect in taxes in 2016 and are expected to decline until exhaustion in 2038, when annual tax income will be able to pay for only about 73 percent of benefits. Over the long term, the OASDI trust funds face an actuarial deficit of 1.86 percent of taxable payroll (based on the intermediate assumptions in the 2001 Trustees Report). (SSA, 2002b)

Many human resource departments do not prioritize this crisis in the business strategies for the organization (Dalton, et al., 1995 ;Dychtwald, 1999). Many of the baby boomers will not be financially and emotionally prepared to retire, thus creating challenges in the workplace (Sunoo, 1997). Human resource departments' retirement training programs often do not address the potential fall of Social Security and Medicare or the emotional aspects of retirement (Thompson, 1999; Ward, 1999). Therefore, some employees heading into retirement are at risk.

The large number of baby boomers expected to retire in the next decade will create labor shortages in many industries (Lach, 1999). Organizations will be challenged as the expertise of the older workers is lost. The challenge is the careful balance of the loss of expertise and the lack of retraining to retain the older worker.

> Policy makers should consider expanding older worker programs and refocusing general employment and training programs to better meet the needs of the impending increase in disadvantaged older workers (Poulos, 1997, p. 45).

The increase in early retirement may lead to the loss of key people needed to maintain the organization (Schweiger, Gosselin, & Lambertucci, 1995). Human resource professionals need to make plans to maintain the organization. This may include redesigning the structure and world of work to accommodate the return of the older worker to the workplace.

Problem Statement

The problem was to determine whether preretirement training programs satisfy the needs of the early retiree in the actual experience of retirement. Interest in early retirement has increased as many baby boomers prepare for retirement. The patterns of early retirement can impact the method organizations use to schedule work hours, succession planning, employee assistance programs, and the specific work life benefits offered to employees. Evidently human resource professionals are unaware of the needs of early retirees; an understanding of the early retiree's experience of retirement can enhance the organization's human resource strategy and planning.

Purpose Statement and Research Questions

This study focused upon the experience of male and female early retirees who have been in retirement for more than one year. The purpose of the study was to explore the process and outcomes of the early retiree in preretirement planning. To accomplish this purpose, the following research questions were proposed.

Research Questions

1. What were the content topics of preretirement training and counseling offered by the early retirees' human resource department?

2. How do preretirement training programs apply to and satisfy the actual needs of the early retiree?

Individuals were interviewed to capture their experience of preretirement training and retirement.

Conceptual Framework

This study compared the experience of human resources' preparation for retirement to the actual retirement experience and then led to the specific topics of the decision-making process through two holistic life models. Therefore, the conceptual framework included a three-tier approach.

The first concept was based upon Lindahl's 1949 study called "What Makes a Good Job?" Lindahl surveyed managers and employees about the 10 key issues to the workers' interests. In the study, the managers and employees responses did not match, thus revealing a gap in potential leadership and strategy initiatives targeted toward employees. Lindahl's study can be reworked today with the issue of human resource planning perceptions between human resource management and the retiring or retired employees. With the current state of human resource offerings for retiring employees, the perception gap and expectations might be similar to the mismatched perceptions of Lindahl's 1949 study. Therefore, it is vital to understand the position of the retiring and retired employees to prepare organizations for the shift in organizational culture created by the increase of early retirees and older workers.

The second concept was built upon Dalton's (1987) holistic concept model of life planning. The holistic model incorporated planning in the areas of health, wealth, recreation, career, companionship, and geography. This model was used as a template for the potential decision-making model within the retirement planning process.

The third concept was obtained from the holistic approach to health and wellness. Hettler (1980) created a model of wellness with six dimensions: physical, occupational, social, spiritual, intellectual, and emotional. Each of these dimensions balanced the individual's internal and external environment. Later, this model evolved into a measurement of lifestyle. This model was also used as a template for decision-making, planning and satisfaction in retirement.

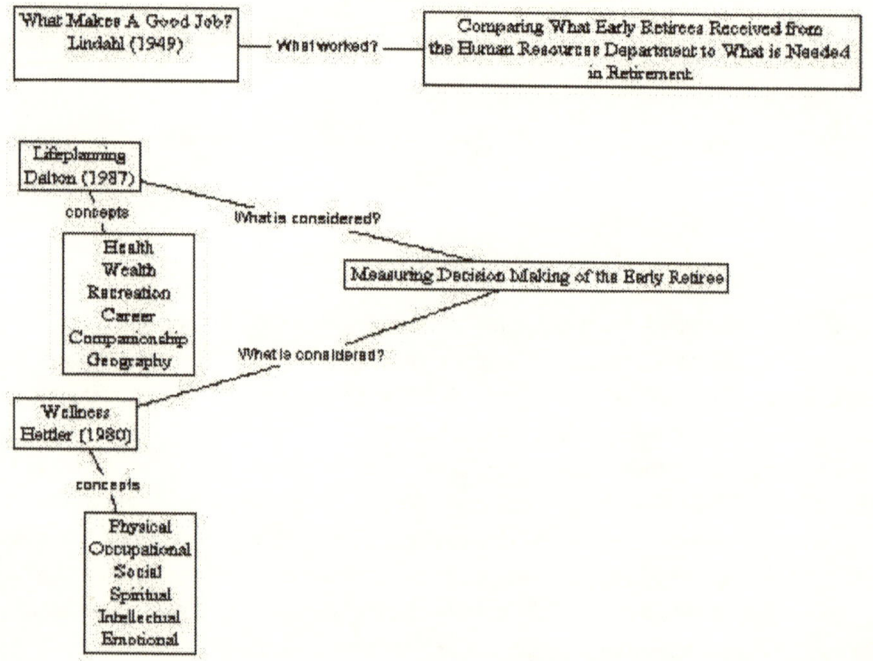

Figure 3. Conceptual framework.

The above models guided the exploration of the research questions within this study to capture the nature of the preparation needed for satisfaction in retirement. Through the holistic exploration of retirement, human resource professionals can be prepared for the baby boomer generation moving toward retirement.

3

Understanding Retirement

A Traditional Definition of Retirement

The traditional definition of retirement has often included the departure from employment with the acceptance of a pension plan (Costa, 1998; Gendell, 2001). Other definitions of retirement have been associated with the changing life events of elderly people (Ekerdt & Clark, 2001; Rosenkoetter & Garris, 2001). Retirement has had an impact on roles and organizations. "Retirement is essentially a social institution implying transition out of another formally recognized social role, that of paid employment" (Walker, 1996, p. 3). With the many definitions of retirement, Ekerdt and DeViney (1993) view retirement as vague and limited with a focus upon only the financial and employment aspects. There has appeared to be a lack of clarity of the definition and measurement of retirement and retirees (Talaga & Beehr, 1995). In one study, the defining characteristics of retirees were usually over the age of 50; spend less of their time working for pay; receive an income designated for retirees; and view themselves as retired (Talaga & Beehr, 1995). With the diversity of definitions and understanding of retirement, researchers have begun to believe that retirement is heading toward a state of change and redefinition (Dychtwald 1999; Garydn, 2000; Stein, 2000; Walker, 1996).

Retirement Redefined

Retirement was initially created as a successful employment transition (Ekerdt & DeViney, 1993) to allow a reward to spend more time to relax and savor the pleasures of family, travel, hobbies, and leisure (Samuelson, 1999). Retirement was for individuals who could afford this, but the nature of retirement has been changing. Gardyn (2000) reported the redefinition of retirement as productive aging where many retirees participate in various activities, including volunteerism, care-giving, educational, skill development, working for pay, and other pursuits considered contributions to society.

The concepts of retirement are changing according to Walker (1996) who views the retirement concepts as

1. an event, a period, a social institution

2. the third age, a new name for retirement?

3. a life-stage within a life-course perspective

4. productive aging

5. a subject of industrial gerontology. (p. 4)

Retirement has many meanings for the retirees and the general population. Gee and Baillie (1999) categorized retirement experiences as a transition to old age/rest, a new beginning, continuity, or a forced, imposed disruption from work. The experiences have been connected to the actual decision-making of retirement. Writers such as Dychtwald (1999) believed retirement could be changing to a more cyclical pattern instead of the traditional pattern of retirement.

In the book *Age Power*, Dychtwald (1999) stated:

> We will cycle in and out of several careers in adulthood, each interspersed with periods of rest, retraining and personal reflection. In addition, rather than saving all of our leisure and retirement for the end of our lives, regular breaks throughout adulthood for recreation will become commonplace. (p. 107)

Stein (2000) supported the new meaning of retirement as a cycle of learning, working, and leisure. His model presented a new pattern for the understanding of the retirement experience of today's retirees. Additionally, Stein (2000) suggested a pattern shift in older adults toward partial retirement with temporary part-time work or self-employment.

Several factors have influenced the new meaning for retirement: the age of retirement, financial viability, health status, and early retirement. Additionally, Dychtwald (1999) asserted the linear life pattern is no longer true and that life patterns are more cyclic. This has been where an individual does not follow a structured pattern of life but experiences nonlinear patterns of work, leisure, and learning. At earlier ages, adults have been drawn to the freedoms within retirement and the ability to pursue lifelong aspirations in a cyclical manner instead of only during the retirement phase. Dychtwald stated that a time of new life pursuits and passions occurs after the age of 45. It appears that retirement has become a rebirth or reinvention of the current lifestyle for the retiree. The reinvention of identity and life in retirement has included more opportunities to expand through learning and the pursuit of new hobbies.

The government has responded to the changes of retirement as the Administration on Aging has created an initiative to focus on retirement for the baby boomers called "Redefining Retirement: The Baby Boomer Challenge" (Dennis & Migliaccio, 1997). The focus of the initiative has been to explore the expectations and needs of the baby boomers and the changes in retirement, and to prepare for the upcoming wave of retirements of this generation. Studies conducted by Moore and Biordi (1995) have suggested the concept of retirement has changed and will continue to do so in the coming years. In one Canadian study, the cause for changes in retirement was associated with the changes in career patterns (Marshall, Clark, & Ballanyne, 2001). The changes within career patterns and the economy were factors in the redefinition of retirement (Drucker, 2001; Kazel, 1998). With the redefinition of retirement in progress, a review the models and process of retirement in the existing literature would be important for further understanding of this study.

Models and Process of Retirement

The models of retirement have lacked clarity regarding roles and responsibilities of the elderly in the 21st century. The abrupt change in life has often been associated with Atchley's (1983) continuity theory as a method of adaptation to retirement and aging. Within the experience of continuity, there are both internal factors, "the persistence of a personal structure of ideas based on memory" (p. 249), and external factors, "living in familiar environments and interacting with familiar people" (p. 249). The impact of continuity has been a decision-making factor within retirement and a means for creation of new social networks, roles, and identities following retirement.

Role theory has been another model for retirement. The theory has viewed retirement as an absence of a role identity and potential role loss (Merton, 1957; Moen, Dempster-McClain, & Williams, 1992; Riley & Riley, 1994). The transition into retirement has been a time to redefine roles in life as the individual departs from a career job. To solve the issue of role loss and to increase retirement satisfaction, the theorists have suggested to maintain role identity by continuing to work after retirement. (Quick & Moen, 1998)

The life course theoretical model for retirement has suggested retirement has been a normal life cycle transition (Elder, 1992). In changing times, the relevance of life course theory could be challenged by the changing demographics of current times (Dychtwald, 1999). Through a combination of the theoretical models of continuity and role theory, the perspective of life course theory for retirement could be enhanced (Quick & Moen, 1998). Changes in career patterns, including part time and contingency work, could change how the life course theory applies to retirement.

Beehr's (1986) theories of the retirement process set the foundation for retirement study. Within the process of retirement, Beehr introduced the individual and organizational outcomes of retirement in several categories. Initially, Beehr discussed the types of retirement as voluntary versus involuntary, partial versus complete, and on-time versus early. Each category was related to the satisfaction and adjustment experience in retirement. The decision-making influences for retirement were presented in Beehr's research as occupational attainment, retirement expectations, financial considerations, personality, and the specific type of profession. All of these factors contributed to the individual's satisfaction within retirement. What remained unclear were the impacts of retiring individuals upon the organization and its specific impact on organizational climate. Beehr's model introduced the many variables available for study as the dynamics of retirement have been changing with demographic shifts. Beehr referred to retirement as a process and proposed the following model considerations.

In the individual consideration for retirement, the internal and external factors in one's life exist in the individual's thinking process about retirement. The planning process of retirement has remained to focus upon the following factors; the individual expectations of retirement, the present state of the individual, health, finances, work life and the pursuit of leisure interests. The process presented by Beehr has continued to be useful in the understanding of retirement.

Section 2:
The Personal and Organizational Experience of Retirement

4

A Holistic Exploration of Retirement

Lifeplanning and Wellness as Models for Preretirement Training

Existing literature does not support a holistic approach to retirement. Therefore, this section will address the concept of life planning and wellness, holistic themes discussed as a potential model for preretirement preparation. The holistic themes that emerged were from studies on the activities of retirees.

Lifeplanning as a Model in Retirement

Dalton's (1987) model of lifeplanning is and incorporates planning in health, wealth, recreation, career, companionship, and geography. Health and wealth have been the top two concerns in preparation and decision making about retirement. The status of the individual's health condition is a major aspect of how and when an individual will retire. The wealth and the health components were of equally important for planning in retirement (Anderson & Weber, 1993). A crucial component of the planning process has been the maintenance of financial resources to care for the retiree and dependents. The next sections will address the lifeplanning model.

Companionship

The term *social support* has been defined as the social relationships throughout the life course that provide contributions to an individual's life (Kahn & Antonucci, 1980). Companionship and social support are related. The social interaction with others within the transition into and following retirement has been important in the individual's satisfaction in retirement (Baker, 2002). Relationships have been a major determinant in the decision-making process. A major influence has been the role of a significant other, marital partner, or family. The partner's work status, companionship, and economics have added into the decision to retire (Henkens, 1999). Gall and Evans (2000) discovered in a study ($\underline{N}$ = 109) the creation of shared retirement times have influenced the decision making around the topic of companionship.

In some ways, individuals have decided to participate as volunteers to maintain a level of contribution and companionship. The participation of adults over the age 55 in volunteerism has had a direct relationship in creating lower mortality rates. A high rate of volunteerism, in two or more organizations, have a positive impact on one's personal health (Oman, Thorsensen, & McMahon, 1999). The participants reported the social support received by fellow volunteers, through keeping track of each other's lives, has provided a reason to continue to live and stay healthy to contribute. As individuals have entered retirement, they often times have felt a need to give back to their community. In Russell Gerbman's (1999) article about companies linking retirees to volunteer work, Jim Whalen of Prudential's Retirees offering Community Service said, "Retirees are looking for meaningful opportunities where they can share their lifetime experiences and skills" (p. 75).

Moen (1998) supported the interest in volunteerism for retirees because the retirees have a need to be connected in meaningful ways. The interest in volunteerism has expanded in organizations that already existed to promote older adult's volunteerism. Several service-oriented programs have offered opportunities to learn, socialize, and build new skills (Moen, 1998). Two programs with opportunities for retirees have been the Foster Grandparents Program and the Retired Seniors Volunteer Program.

Corporations and organizations have become involved in retiree volunteer programs. Many corporate retiree volunteer programs have been formed with both governmental and independent support. Civic Ventures is a San Francisco-based organization that has supported older adults entering social service volunteerism. The Experience Corps of Civic Ventures has attracted older adults to participate in service to communities (Gardyn, 2000).

The Corporation for National Service created the Senior Corps, which includes the Foster Grandparent Program, The Retired and Service Volunteer Program and the Senior Companion Program. These programs have government connections to the Domestic Volunteer Service Act of 1973. Additionally, the Senior Corps was built under the belief that community needs can be met by the resources provided by senior volunteers (Corporation for National Service, 2001).

The National Retiree Volunteer Coalition has continued as another organization that has trained corporations to create corporate retiree volunteer programs (Smith, 1994). Donna Anderson, the president of the National Retiree Volunteer Coalition, has stated, "This program represents a whole new approach to valuing retirement. The idea of NRVC is to transfer work skills to community leadership" (quoted in Smith, 1994, p. 7).

Another example of older Americans' contributions is the creation of Hope Meadows in Rantoul, Illinois. Sociologist Brenda Erhart created the community of families that include seniors serving as foster grandparents to children in the foster care system. Hope Meadows is a community that was transformed from an abandoned Illinois Air Force base. "Sixty of the buildings were purchased from the Pentagon by Generations of Hope, a nonprofit corporation" (Smith, 2001, p. 10). These buildings were turned into Hope Meadow, a residential community that houses "Hope" families with foster children and housing for seniors on fixed incomes. "The seniors agree to volunteer for at least six hours a week in service to Hope's children and families, in exchange for low monthly rents in the $300–$400 range" (p. 11). The seniors have served as volunteers in many capacities, "neighbors, tutors, baby-sitters, crossing guards, play ground monitors, bicycle repairmen, mentors, role models, and friends to the parents and their children" (p. 10). It has been through the creative multigenerational programs, like Hope Meadows, and the cultural dynamics of the United States that will have continued advancements with the contributions of the retiree.

In the year 2000, 44% of American seniors volunteered, according to Bradley (2000). Again, volunteerism has continued as a means to support the spiritual aspect of wellness for the retiree. The statistic of volunteerism has been on the rise with the largest contribution coming from the baby boomer generation. The motivation behind volunteerism has been (a) providing an enhanced sense of purpose, (b) increased personal growth, and (c) continued productivity (Bradley, 2000).

The increase in volunteerism has represented another shift at the understanding of retirement. The mentioned organizations have created a plan to use the valuable resources retirees can provide to society. Organizational efforts to support volunteerism as individuals retire will have continued the creation of a new cultural shift for retirement. The shift to include volunteerism in retirement has been supported by both government and private innovations.

Health

In some decision-making models, health has been one of the determining factors of whether or not to retire (Beehr, 1986). Hummer's (1999) study creates a link between health behaviors and religious involvement facilitated through the healthy lifestyle proscription of many denominations, reducing certain health risk factors. Some lifestyle aspects of denominations include the limited or no use of alcohol and certain dietary rules that lead to healthier lifestyles. The shift to positive health behaviors increased positive well-being in retirement (Lo & Brown, 1999). Additionally, in the study conducted by Rosenkotter, Garris, & Endahl (2001) the participants ($\underline{N}$ = 764) reported more positive health behaviors, such as the reduction of alcohol, in retirement. Such studies support the concepts of Dalton's lifeplanning within the realm of improved health. Health-related behaviors are a concern for retirees in the planning for retirement.

Wealth

Economic well being has remained as one of the major decision-making points within retirement (Atchley, 1983; Beehr, 1986; Feldman, 1994). The financial retirement incentives offered by organizations have been an influence in the decision-making process. The careful planning for a specific standard of living in retirement has eased the adjustment into retirement.

However, some people have not been financially ready to retire at the stated retirement age. A key aspect of the impact of financial retirement goals of the baby boomer population has been the lack of information (Schieber, 1996). The economic downturn created by the investment collapse in 2002 will have an adverse effect on the uninformed retiree. Who should be responsible for retirement planning, the employer or the employee? Many individuals do not know how much money they will need in retirement, how to save for retirement, or the level of investment risks they should be taking (Schieber, 1996). Therefore, a focus upon wealth planning has been a vital aspect to the retirement planning and decision-making process.

Career

The career aspect of retirement has continued to unfold as more retirees have been returning to accept other employment following retirement. Some may have served as consultants or some may have started new careers. Over one third of retirees returned to work, some for financial reasons, others have returned for the structure and social interaction it provides (Hurd, 1995).

Bridge employment, part-time/temporary work or self-employment, has also occurred within retirement. "Bridging is a form of partial retirement in which an older worker alternates periods of disengagement from the workplace with periods of temporary, part-time, occasional, or self-employed work" (Stein, 2000, p. 1). Stein (2000) reported three main reasons individuals participate in bridge employment: financial need, liking to work, and keeping busy. Retirement employment may support the concepts within the lifeplanning model for retirement.

Wellness as a Model in Retirement

Hettler (1980) created a model of wellness with six dimensions: physical, occupational, social, spiritual, intellectual and emotional. Hettler's holistic model of wellness encompassed some of the retirement planning, decision-making, and activities presented in current literature. Hettler's definitions of the wellness dimension are listed below.

1. Spiritual–seeking meaning and purpose in human existence.

2. Occupational–preparation for work in which one will gain personal satisfaction and find enrichment in one's life

3. Social–contributing to one's human and physical environment for the common welfare of community

4. Physical–encouragement of cardiovascular flexibility and strength through regular physical activity

5. Intellectual–encourages creative, stimulating mental activities

6. Emotional—awareness of one's feelings (Hettler, 1980).

The concepts of the wellness model in retirement will be explored further in this section.

Spiritual

The concept of aging and spiritual growth has started the creation of many programs across the country in spiritual eldering or saging. The models in spiritual eldering have fostered intergenerational mentoring and embraced the talents and contributions of older adults (Leder, 2000). Intergenerational mentoring has become a transitional return to respecting elders versus a culture afraid of aging. This transition has allowed for more retirees to express wisdom to other generations, similar to Erikson's generativity (1982) and Fowler's (1981) fifth stage of service. Additionally, a continuation of religious involvement has been connected to a decrease in adult mortality (Hummer, 1999).

A shift has occurred within the individuals as they age and make decisions about retirement. In the past, the elder has been able to reduce life commitments and basically disengage in life (Leder, 2000). However, today's spiritual focus has presented a new paradigm to a focus on transcendence. Erikson (1982) and Leder (2000) both have discussed this time as a loss of the ego self, a greater sense of peace, and a connection to a higher being. The experience has often occurred in midlife, with career pursuits, earning money, and raising family, where the individual has lost this sense of greater being (Leder, 2000). However, with the emergence of early retirements and forced retirements, individuals have experienced a shift within the spiritual realm of one's life. Some individuals have contemplated the importance of work in the role of life, especially during midlife, and as the individuals contemplate retirement. The retirement process may include a spiritual growth experience.

As an introduction to the experience of spirituality, Scott Peck (1994) presented the word *crisis* that is often associated with the mid-life crisis. Peck supported the psychospiritual work necessary to resolve the conflict issues of the midlife crisis. Peck believed the fear of aging has been what has impacted the progression through midlife crisis. Many times an individual entering retirement has experienced the grief and loss process of Kubler-Ross (1969) in the book *On Death and Dying*. The stages of grief are denial, anger, negotiation, depression, and acceptance. Although Kubler-Ross did not recognize it at the time, the most fascinating thing about this is that we go through exactly the same stages in exactly the same order any time we make any significant step in our psychological or spiritual growth (Peck, 1993, p. 64).

In one area of spiritual growth, many individuals have experienced the process of forgiveness. "A big part of growing up is learning to forgive. We go through life blaming others for our pain. And blame always begins with anger" (Peck, 1993, p. 29). Forgiveness has been part of the process of retirement in forced and involuntary retirements. Peck believed forgiveness was for the individuals' own healing, freedom from the past, and allowed for growth in an individual's well being. As an individual grows through the retirement process, an opening may occur for further spiritual growth and contribution.

The idea of spiritual eldering or intergenerational mentoring has continued to evolve with the older adults of all religious traditions in the United States. Leder (2000) in his residence at the Chicago Park Ridge Center for the Study of Health, Faith and Ethics designed a model for a "hypothetical ElderSpirit Center" that has provided spiritually oriented classes, retreats, resources, and guidance for visitors and affiliates. A movement within many religious traditions has been to engage the older adults in continued involvement in the community.

Rabbi Zalman Schachter-Shalomi with the Alliance for Jewish Renewal formed the Spiritual Eldering Institute in 1989 (Leder, 2000). The processes conducted in the Spiritual Eldering Institute allowed individuals to conduct a healing life review to release unresolved issues, create plans for embracing life as an elder, and to share wisdom (Schater-Shalomi & Miller, 1995). It has been through the movement of spiritual traditions that many fully embraced the older adult into society. The ideas of intergenerational mentoring, with the wisdom from elders, has been a movement of inclusion and societal shifts embracing retirees. Leder (2000) asserted these programs allow an expression of traditional elder wisdom in the response to contemporary needs of society.

In many ways, some retirees have proceeded through a variety of spiritual choices as the individuals have prepared and entered retirement. Often in retirement, grief and spiritual growth have occurred leading to an identity transformation for the individual (Leder, 2000). Retirees also may have chosen to become active contributors through spiritual eldering and intergenerational mentoring programs.

Intellectual

As the population has aged, more people have been interested in intellectual pursuits and lifelong learning. (Eisen, 1998) As a result, organizations have been preparing for an increase in the number of retirees entering the learning environment. The blended life cycle of today has distributed learning, work, and leisure over the course of life (Eisen, 1998; Stein, 2000). The intellectual dimension is present in retirement. Over 300 U.S. colleges have established "learning in retirement" programs to meet the older adult's need to be intellectually challenged (Gardyn, 2000). Colleges are already enrolling mature students, and this will be enhanced with more elder students entering learning environments. Retired individuals have been returning to the classroom to receive degrees, participating in travel learning groups such as Elderhostel, learning how to start a business, or trying a new hobby. The education market has been responding by creating elder colleges and learning in retirement programs to support this growing population.

Universities across the country have created new ways to meet the need of the retiree who has returned to learning. Northwestern University in Evanston, Illinois, created the Learning in Retirement program, which serves many retired learners (Northwestern University, 2002). These learning communities have enhanced knowledge and built community relations.

Often retirees enroll in learning environments to start entirely new careers or to gain additional training in an interest area. Some city-related centers for aging have focused upon the retraining of older adults, specifically in computer skills training (Poulos, 1997). With new computer skills, older adults have returned to the workforce (Czaja, 2001). The retirees have returned to learning for the enhancement of the life.

Occupational

An occupational dimension of life has been supported in retirement research. Choosing to work in retirement has supported not only the financial aspect, but has enhanced continuity (Atchley, 1983) and role identification (Kim & Feldman, 2000). Retirees have wanted to work later in life after retirement. With the increase in lifespan, working in retirement has supported the greater output in life with a human capital contribution continuing into older ages (Swanson & Kopekcy, 1999).

Retirees have returned to the workforce. Although older workers are retiring from their regular jobs at earlier ages, many are continuing to participate in the labor market in some way after their retirement (Kim & Feldman, 2000). With the growing number of older people over 50, Drucker (2001) predicted that the older worker will not keep working full-time. Instead, the older worker will work in the roles of a temporary, part-time worker and as a consultant. One option for retirees has been bridge employment.

As the number of older workers has risen, a few corporations have created opportunities to invite the older worker to the corporation. "Travelers Insurance has taken a leadership role in using older workers by creating a job bank of temporary employees from a pool of retirees. The higher productivity of these workers has saved Travelers $1.5 million a year" (Dychtwald, 1999, p. 106). The CEO of Bonne Bell, Jess A. Bell, at age 74 created the "Seniorsonly" production group for the cosmetic company (Dychtwald, 1999). It has been these innovations in hiring practices that have led other organizations to utilize the skills and talents of the older workers in America. Dychtwald (1999) called this new innovation "rehirement" instead of retirement (p. 106). Dychtwald (1999) hoped that the new hiring practices of these organizations will destroy the "silver-ceiling" that has limited employment for the aging population. As more organizations have desired retirees to return to the workforce, human resource planners have created a need to further define the needs of the organization to accommodate these workers. A benefit to the organization has been the exploration of expertise the retired individual has brought to the organization.

One important perspective to the human resource department of an organization has been the lower cost of training an older worker versus a younger worker. With the seasoned experience of an older worker, the training time and costs have been greatly reduced (Kiefer & Briner, 1998). "General Electric has discovered that it is more economical to retrain veteran engineers in emerging technologies than to hire new ones" (Dychtwald, 1999, p. 106). The promotion of the older worker's experience in the notion of reduced training time has further encouraged organizations to hire the more seasoned employee (Purcell, 2000). As more corporations have promoted the cost savings benefit from hiring seasoned workers, the retiree with expanded experience has continued and expanded opportunities for bridge employment in various fields of work. Through these options, retirees have continued to contribute to the workplace, and organizations have benefited from a skilled employee. Kiefer and Briner (1998) supported the use of retirees for training to keep important knowledge and skills in the organization. To summarize, recent trends in retirement have included second careers, volunteering for social causes, continuing education, and different types of work for pay (Gardyn, 2000). These trends are all related to the occupational aspect of wellness.

5

What is the HR Role in Preparing the Boomers for Retirement?

Human Resource Management History and Theory

The early developments of human resource management that built the field were scientific management, welfare work, and industrial psychology (Dulebohn, Ferris, & Stodd, 1995). Through the early studies of management, the employee relationship to the employer needed further study for its impact on productivity. In 1913, Munsterberg (as cited in Dulebohn, Ferris, & Stodd, 1995) supported the need for an applied field of psychology that would study areas of employment testing, selection, training, worker adjustment, efficiency, and motivation. The field of human resource management was created.

The development of theories for human resource management has been challenging to academics and practitioners. "To date, the focus of researchers on individual HRM functions and activities has resulted in a failure to develop an integrative theory of HRM" (Ferris, Barnum, Rosen, Holleran, & Dulebohn, 1995, p. 3). The lack of theory has been partially created by the relationship between academics and practitioners. The perception of HRM practitioners has been academic research does not apply to the workplace. (Ferris, Barnum, Rosen, Holleran, & Dulebohn, 1995). The field of human resource management continues to expand as a profession and as an important business strategy. However, researchers are slow to create models and theories for the human resource management field. Ferris, Barnum, Rosen, Holleran, and Dulebohn (1995) have stated:

> Therefore, while the evolution of the practice of HRM-from a maintenance function to a one of increasing organizational and strategic importance-has

30

resulted in an integration of activities in HRM practice, the science of HRM has been marked by an absence of an integrative theory or general conceptual system. (p. 3)

To expand HRM research and theories, a combination of science and practical application needs to occur with the increased interactions between researchers and practitioners. The gap between researchers and practitioners has created a slow response to theory building for the field of human resource management.

Human resource professionals manage all the aspects of the employee-to-employer relationship. LeRoy and Schultz (1995) suggested the roles of human resource professionals within a legal context as the advocate, protector, lobbyist, and whistleblower. These roles shift between varying allegiances to the organization and the employee. The difficult task has been to identify one role for the human resource professional and to include the other topics of organizational psychology, organizational sociology, industrial relations, human relations, and strategic management (Ferris, Rosen, & Barnum, 1995). Additionally, the human resource professional must balance the topics of equal opportunity, job analysis, training and development, labor relations, performance evaluation, and compensation (Ivancevich, 1998).

With the differences in roles and the lack of theory, a definition of human resource management has been created.

> Human resource management is the science and the practice that deals with the nature of the employment relationship and all of the decisions, actions, and issues that related to that relationship. In practice, it involves an organization's acquisition, development, and utilization of employees, well as the employees' relationship to an organization and its performance. (Ferris, Barnum, Rosen, Holleran & Dulebohn, 1995, pp. 1–2)

Human resource management professionals are in conflict with the academic researchers of the field, creating a gap in solid research for areas of organizational interest. The understanding of this difficult relationship supports the need for further studies of human resource management to develop theories and solutions for organizations. An understanding of the human resource management profession leads to the opportunity to explore retirement as a human resource issue.

Human Resource Perspectives of Retirement

The human resource perspective of retirement is vital to meeting the legal requirements under the Employee Retirement Income Security Act of 1974 (Duleboh, Ferris, & Stodd, 1995). There are many factors that influence human resource retirement decision making about individuals heading into retirement within organizations. On one side of the coin, allowing older workers to remain in the workforce creates stability and encourages expertise to remain in the organization. On the other side, later retirement, specifically of university faculty members, has reduced the opportunity for younger faculty, women, and minorities to access positions, revealed in a study of faculty members ($\underline{N}$ = 500) over the age of 56 (Bahrami, 2001).

In the onset of retirement legislation, the employer carried the responsibility of retirement planning for the employee; however, retirement planning has now shifted from the employer to the employee (Hurd, 1995). In a recent survey conducted by HR Focus (2001), more than half of those surveyed had specific goals regarding the employment of older workers, and few had developed a plan to manage early retirements of those who are reaching the age of 55. Past research only provided a limited view of retirement with its focus on retirement decision-making process as a rational, economic choice driven by health (Sullivan, 1992). With the limited understanding of retirement, it has been difficult for human resource professionals to plan for the needs of individuals preparing to retire. Human resource professionals have needed more information about the retirement decision-making process to plan effective preretirement training and benefit programs.

Human resource professionals have responded to a changing economy and structure of the world of work. Moen (1998) had stated the restructuring of work has been a consequence of the development of a more global economy, technological change, the shift to a service economy, and concerns over productivity and competitiveness. The changes in how organizations compete in the marketplace have played a major role in an emphasis on the younger worker versus the older worker. Older workers have been perceived as not open to a changing environment forcing some organizations to focus upon the younger employee (Wellner, 1999).

The human resource professional not only has to learn to understand the planning and decision making of the early retiree, but also needs to link the impact of the retirees' departure to business strategy. Some organizations are choosing to reduce costs by offering early retirement incentives. Although it reduces costs, it has appeared that "there has been no attention to that turnover that is deliberately generated by the organization" (Dalton et al., 1995, p. 620). Organizations have not been investigating the impact of the early retiree turnover rates. The organizations could be losing talent that could impact the organizations' profitability.

> One popular way to reduce staff is to offer early retirement incentives. The hope here is that a sufficiently large number of employees will "voluntarily" exit, serving to meet the downsizing targets set for each effected business unit. The other hope is that the employees choosing to leave will not be the most valued employees. (Dreher & Kendall, 1995, p. 452)

Organizations might question the impact of organizational culture and organizational change that often occurs following downsizing.

> Methods that utilize voluntary turnover (e.g. attrition, early retirement) may create less trauma than those that do not. Voluntary approaches however, can be problematic. For example, early retirement incentives may lead to over subscription. Both early retirement and attrition may lead to the premature loss of key people needed to build a new organization. (Schweiger, Gosselin, & Lambertucci, 1995, p. 306)

Human resource professionals appear to not be monitoring the increasing number of early retirees and the impact on the organization. Researchers and practitioners are not exploring the changing demographics and corporate environment that has created an increase in early retirement.

> A second illustration of deliberate turnover which has received very little attention (for a notable exception, see Feldman 1994) and might be rightfully interpreted as yet another example of resizing the firm, is early retirement programs. The research that has been conducted–largely in gerontology and demography-has focused on factors which may predict why an individual might elect to accept early retirement and how that decision affects early retirees. We are aware of no research, however, which addresses whether early retirement programs, or aspects of early retirement programs are related to firm productivity or profitability. There seems to be no information on whether such programs are associated with competitive advantage within industries. Given the ubiquity of such programs, we can sympathize with the disappointment of some HRM professionals when considering the development of conceptualization and research in this area (Dalton, 1995, p. 621).

This section has supported the need for new understandings of retirement and early retirement for human resource professionals.

Planning for Retirement and Preretirement Training

In some organizations the human resource departments have offer lectures and meetings to assist employees' decision making about retirement planning. However, the plans and types of preretirement training have been inconsistent. Hunter (1980) designed a comprehensive preretirement training program that included topics of work, physical health, mental health, retirement income, financial planning, employment, consumer information, housing, social relationships, legal concerns, leisure time, widowhood, death, and dying and sexuality. Hunter's design was to match the current times and life cycle patterns. The more current focus of preretirement discussions with the employee has been upon the financial and health benefits for the time after the employee has retired. Retirement planning has been explained in two models, limited and comprehensive. The limited model explained pensions, timing and benefits. The comprehensive model explained the limited model topics and added mental health, housing, leisure activities, legal activities and financial planning (Atchley, 1983). "Thus far, the need for retirement preparation is not being met for the vast majority of people" (p. 225).

As the population of the United States has been experiences an aging workforce, a new focus has been created upon retirement planning. In studies of the preretirement process, older male workers displayed changes in values, identity, behavior, and realigned relationships with family, friends and coworkers (Ekerdt & DeViney, 1993). Financial planners have explored the expansion of the services for retirement planning to include other aspects of life to accompany financial planning. Bradley (2002) stated a structured retirement workshop for preretirees should have included other professionals such as a real estate agent, a therapist, a community volunteer, a senior health care professional, a CPA, and an attorney. Additionally, Bradley stated that a preretirement workshop address the human experience of retirement. The topics that should be covered include where to live, how to spend time, the marriage with more time spent together, and new family traditions. Further, in a study by Gee and Baillie (1999) about retirement expectations, the top findings for preretirement training were financial management, hobbies, and physical health with community resources and learning as follow up topics. These studies support a more well-rounded preretirement training program for many organizations. With the many suggestions of the topics and planning for retirement, the experience of the retiree might be considered a useful method in determining the content for preretirement training.

The Legal Aspects Impacting Human Resource Departments

Legal issues impact the function and tasks of human resource departments. One major legal aspect that has been guided by the government was the quality of worklife. The concern for physical and psychological quality of worklife was influenced by three government acts (a) the Civil Rights Act of 1964, (b) The Occupational Safety and Health Act of 1970, (c) Employee Retirement Income Security Act of 1974 (Duleboh, Ferris, & Stodd, 1995). The human resource issue of retirement was greatly influenced by government regulation.

The ERISA Act of 1974, within the Department of Labor, provided governance for businesses' administration and regulation of pension programs offered as an employee benefit (Department of Labor, 2003). ERISA was designed to ensure employees were provided with the pension benefits that were promised when the individual retired. A few of the regulations and issues of compliance under the ERISA include a requirement for definition of eligibility for a pension program, the management and disbursement of pension plans, and protection for other retirement benefits agreed upon by the company.

Under employment law regarding retirement benefits, the key issue is to protect the retired employee. Human resource departments are challenged to comply with the ERISA regulations combined with the IRS regulations on retirement benefits (Department of Labor, 2003). The guidance of ERISA requires businesses that offer pension programs to provide detailed information about the plans to the employees (Illinois Law, 2003) but the information is often provided at the early stages of an individual's employment at an organization.

As human resource professionals are being challenged for not offering many planning services for retirees, the concern has rested within the legalities of offering programs without risk. A current policy topic with potential impacts upon human resource departments has been Social Security reform. With the prediction by some politicians of Social Security depletion in the near future, human resource professionals and professional organizations have been busy gathering legal information to protect the organization from potential lawsuits. The first issue of concern has been the potential privatization of the Social Security system which will have placed more responsibility on the employer to manage the new "personal retirement accounts" (Thompson, 1999). Another aspect of reform has included the increase of payroll tax for employers. The employers may have to increase pension contributions to compensate for reduced Social Security benefits (Ward, 1999). Human resource professionals have been also concerned over the increase in cost to manage the new private pension programs and the increase in tax burden to the younger Americans in the workforce. The situation has created a financial risk for the organization.

The fallout of Enron Corporation's retirement plans in 2002 leaving many without any retirement savings has intimidated the human resource professionals responsible for providing financial retirement guidance (Castellano, 2002; Cauldron, 2002). In the Enron ripoff, employees were strongly encouraged to place retirement funds completely in Enron stock. Now, many human resource departments are concerned about the legalities of advising employees about financial decision making in retirement. Therefore, the Society for Human Resource Management has made a statement of support for a partnership with government to educate investors if privatization of Social Security reform occurs (Thompson, 1999). Other human resource departments have dealt with the problem by offering financial counseling vouchers to employees to lower the legal risk of retirement planning (Raphael, 2002).

The legal risks of retirement planning, specifically in the area of finances, have continued to slow down human resource departments as they respond to the need for education about retirement. As the baby boomers head toward retirement, the need for education has increased with further support needed from policy makers to protect human resource professionals. Within the past year, Senators Jeff Binaman and Susan Collins have presented a bill, S.R. 1677, to allow human resource professionals to invite outside investors into the organization without being liable for the advice provided (Raphael, 2002). A government approach to further protect organizations in the realm of retirement planning and education may encourage more human resource departments to provide these services.

The Future of the Changing Dynamics of Retirement

In the 1995 White House Conference on Aging, the discussion encompassed the impact of the increasing aged society on individuals, families, health and social services, businesses, government, and the volunteer sector (Pillemer et al., 1995). The discussion implied the potential need for policy makers to become involved in the understanding of retirement in the United States. Samuelson (1999) and Drucker (2001) supported changes in public policies regarding retirement and the creation of new models for corporations to create flexible employment for older workers. The aspects of organizational culture could be assessed in response to the increases in early retirement and older workers in the workplace. More formalized facilitation and socialization has been needed to integrate the individual's experience in the process of retirement (Lindbo & Schultz, 1998). Additionally, the methods to attract and retain older workers in organizations have included switching to a phased retirement system, workplace flexibility, reducing workweeks to a few days per week, and flexible spending accounts (Hayes & Parker, 1993).

Moen (1998) presented three trends impacting the baby boomers and their families, employers and the economy, and for American society. These trends are as follows

> (a) economic and corporate transformations in the workforce and workplace (b) the dramatic increases in longevity and health of those in their 50's, 60's and 70's along with the remarkable turnaround in retirement timing and work exits and reentries; and (c) disjunctive shifts in both gender roles and the family. (Moen, 1998, p. 42)

All of these factors have impacted organizations and the retiree. The changing dynamics of retirement have impacted the organization and the individual. As the baby boomers are head toward retirement, the world of work and retirement may shift.

6

The Retirees' Journey

This is the story of several cases of early retirees living within the metropolitan Chicago area. The data for this exploratory case study were collected through the use of interviews. It is the story of their experience of preretirement training, preparation for retirement and their actual experience of retirement. The sections discuss the research questions and the areas of further exploration within this exploratory case study.

The first section of the chapter presents the answers to research question one, which pertained to the actual preretirement training, and the topics each of the early retirees received from their organizations before retirement. The second section of the data presents the answers to research question two, which pertained to the actual planning needs each early retiree addressed before retirement and modeled under the lifeplanning and wellness conceptual framework. The third section presents the data of further exploration related to planning for retirement and the experience of retirement. The data presented in section three relates to the topic of retirement and pose potential areas of exploration for further study.

This section will present a brief summary of the composite answers of the participants with the study. The composite tables for each interview are located in the appendix. The composites were developed through documenting of each of the participant's answers to the questions in the interviews. After each composite was compiled into a table for each participant, the researcher then assessed the participant comments to create a snapshot of the participants' answers compared to the research questions. The study participants' answers have been summarized in one table within this chapter. The content of the first segment will relate to Research Question 1 regarding the topics for preretirement training.

Section 1: Research Question 1

What were the content topics of preretirement training and counseling offered by the early retirees' human resource department? In section 1, the questions that were discussed with each of the early retirees included various potential preretirement training topics and preretirement counseling offered by the early retirees' organizations. The paragraphs to follow discuss the topics the early retirees received in preretirement training. The composite of the interviews for each participant is located in the appendix.

The first participant was Jim. He retired as a vice president of a large corporation at the age of 51. Jim retired early to pursue a second career and returned to his family, in response to significant health issues. Jim's experience in preretirement training revealed executives in the organization he retired from were offered additional outside services such as legal and financial planning for individuals retiring.

The second participant, Roy, retired at age 63. He was a professor from a community college where the organization offered a large bonus incentive to older professors to encourage them to retire early. Within Roy's composite of preretirement training, the community college offered Roy information about the financial, retirement program offered by the state retirement system, and the health benefits offered to retirees. Roy said that some of the content topics were not needed in preretirement training in his experience because he planned with sources outside of the organization.

Steve's experience of retirement at the age of 47 was that of a retired Air Force officer. The process of preretirement training experience for Steve varied in comparison with the other participants because the military retirement transition program offered more topics than the other participants experienced.

Steve's experience is unique among the 10. The military transition program offered information on a majority of the topics investigated in this study. The components of both legal, financial, and health benefits were presented in Steve's preretirement program. An interesting quality of his program included the focus on the preparation for second careers through offerings of career coaching, resume writing, job searching, and interviewing.

Bill's experience is that of a retired vice president of a major corporation at the age of 58. The position Bill held was under redesign and the organization was under restructuring creating the desire for Bill's early retirement. He experienced various information from his corporation to prepare for retirement.

In Bill's experience of preretirement training, the majority of topics in this study were presented. Although the experience of preretirement training included many of the topics, some of the topics were only presented through reading materials such as booklets and packets of information.

John was experiencing his second retirement, at the age of 56, when interviewed for this study. At this time, he retired as a chief financial officer for a smaller company. Therefore, due to size of his organization, the topics of preretirement training were limited. John's perspective was that many of the topics of preretirement training presented in this study were personal issues the individual had to deal with and that it was not an organizational responsibility.

Mary retired at the age of 55 as a nurse from a local hospital. Her work was varied between full-and part-time work in nursing. With this work structure, Mary's experience of preretirement training did not include many topics. Mary's experience represents the limited amount of benefits offered to a woman in a transitional career. It appears some women vary work commitments to fulfill the many roles women experience in life. Therefore, Mary only experienced a financial gain from her consistent work at a local hospital. All other preretirement preparation topics were ignored as she retired.

Cathy retired at the age of 53 with the background of a variety of administrative roles within several organizations. In her experience as a mother, working was fit in between running a household and raising children. Her financial contribution was to support the academic pursuits and needs of her children. Cathy's responses reveal a traditional view of retirement with no intentions of returning to the workforce in retirement. She also received no assistance in planning for her own retirement from her retiring organization.

Marlene's experience of preretirement training offered by the organization represents another view of the lack of organizational preparation from the human resource departments. Marlene retired in her mid-50s from a major corporation in the administrative field to pursue a doctoral degree and a second career. Marlene represents the pattern in this study, as shown in the summary table later in this chapter, where women appear to not receive much or any preretirement preparation information. In Marlene's responses, she reveals her impression that the planning topics are of individual responsibility instead of organizational responsibility. She revealed that she received coaching to deal with the topics from self-employed individuals and specialized professionals.

Janice's early retirement at age 51 was as a senior vice president for an international travel company. She retired early to enjoy life and do things she did not have time enjoy while being in the corporate world. Although Janice was an executive in the organization, the organization offered minimal assistance for preretirement training compared to the retired male executives in this study. Janice received no guidance from the organization pertaining to preretirement planning or training. Janice explained that the organization was not prepared for her early retirement. The researcher of this study finds it inconsistent with the experience of the retired male executives in this study.

Anna's retirement story was based on her desire to obtain a flexible work schedule to assist her daughter's childcare issues as she returned to work after maternity leave. Anna asked her employer for a part-time, flexible work schedule and her employer, a private high school, denied her request. Her only choice was to retire early from the organization at age 57. Anna's experience matches the preretirement training of the other women in this study. Anna received no training or preparation from the organization. She did have another part-time position in addition to her full-time position that carried her into retirement that included health benefits and allowed her to still work. Anna kept her promise to her daughter and retired early to care for her grandchildren.

Summary of Themes in Preretirement Training

In summarizing the themes of preretirement training, the following table reveals the main topics: financial, with one third of the participants also experiencing the topics of estate planning, will preparation, and health benefits.

Table 2
Summary of Preretirement Training Topics.

	Financial	Estate Planning	Will Preparation	Power of Attny	Eldercare Planning	Resume Writing	Health Benefits	Technology	Career Coaching
Jim	X	X	X						
Roy	X				X		X		
Steve	X		X	X		X	X		X
Bill	X	X	X	X	X	X	X		
John	X	X							
Mary									
Cathy									
Marlene	X								
Janice									
Anna									

The themes of preretirement training in this study reveal the lack of preparation and training offered by a variety of organizations' human resource departments. It appeared the male retired executives were offered more services and content areas for preretirement training compared to the women in this study. Only one woman received any preretirement training, and she received only financial information. Some organizations even offered vouchers and private preretirement planning services for the retired male executives. One might first address the topic of gender differences in these findings. The issues of gender differences could be created by variation of some women's careers in this study. Two of the women reported job changes and variations of full time and part time work to raise children throughout their career. Additionally, the variation in services could be caused by the size of the retirees' organization. The larger organizations appeared to offer more services for preretirement compared to the smaller organizations.

The category of technology in preretirement training was not presented at all in the participants' experience. This is curious since many of the participants reported a greater use of technology in retirement to keep in touch with friends and family members. One reported that he had wished he had more technology training before he retired and it has limited him from obtaining second career positions. Another participant reported taking computer classes as a college before he retired to keep up to date with the increase in use of technology.

There appears to be confusion between what the organization is responsible for in preretirement training compared to the early retiree's perception. The question to answer in this situation would be the organizational versus individual responsibility for preretirement training. What does the organization need to provide in the benefits program for early retirees? All of the participants reported preparation and changes in retirement in the topics listed in the above table. However, some of the participants did state that the issues were of personal nature and did not require the organization's coaching.

Eldercare planning was a topic not presented very often within the preretirement training of the early retirees in this study. The conflict in this situation is the current increase of human resource departments including eldercare services in their benefit packages. The need for eldercare services is increasing within many organizations as more employees are caring for their parents. This can impact organizational productivity.

The topic of career coaching and resume writing did not appear in preretirement training even though 8 of the 10 participants reported working in retirement or starting second careers. The individual that retired from the military reported coaching and guidance for a second career after retirement. In the new meaning of retirement (Stein, 2000), the retirees often cycle through periods of leisure, learning and work. This suggests a need for career coaching and resume writing prior to retirement.

It appeared that with the exception of two individuals, most of the participants did not receive information or benefits regarding health plans in retirement. Many of the participants reported finding other means to find a secure plan for health benefits in retirement. This is incongruent with the priorities of preretirement training, through ERISA, that mainly include financial preparation and health benefits regulations.

Although several organizations have reported offering preretirement training and planning for financial needs, the early retirees of this study reported this topic was presented through booklets and short trainings. All of the participants reported taking care of financial planning for retirement with individual professionals and outside sources. Six of the 10 individuals in this study reported receiving information for financial planning in retirement but it was very limited.

Summary of Research Question 1

Within the topics presented in this study, linked to the theoretical model, the main topic presented by the organization's human resource department was financial planning. The three other topics presented most frequently were estate planning, will preparation, and health benefits but less than half of the participants received information on these topics. A few other topics were presented, such as power of attorney, eldercare planning, resume writing and career coaching but were only experienced by one or two participants in each situation. With the data presented in this study, the only topic covered by the organization was the financial aspects of retirement. All other topics were not presented in preretirement training. As the demographics and the world of work are changing within the United States, the preparation for retirement will become a wider topic of discussion. The above data support Research Question 1, which inquired about the topics presented in preretirement training. The bottom line is what they received from the human resource department in preretirement training was insufficient to what they needed in retirement.

Section 2: Research Question 2

How do preretirement training programs apply to and satisfy the actual needs of the early retiree? In Section 2, the research question is discussed through questions that reflect the conceptual framework of the study. However, given the nature of the interviews, instrument, and the way the study was conducted the researcher was not able to directly answer the question.

The first conceptual framework, based on Lindal's (1947) study, compared the perception of the needs of workers by managers and the actual reported needs of the workers. In this study of preretirement, the participants were asked about content topics that were presented in preretirement training and what they actually needed in retirement. The second, Dalton's (1987) model of life planning with areas of health, wealth, recreation, career, companionship, and geography, and the third conceptual framework, Hettler's (1980) model of wellness with six dimensions, physical, occupational, social, spiritual, intellectual and emotional, were blended in the interview to assess what the early retiree did plan for and needed as a preretirement training topic.

The first component of the research question asked about the application of preretirement training to the actual needs of the early retiree. In the first segment of answering the question and in reviewing the tables under Research Question 1, the following preretirement topics did apply to the early retiree: financial planning, estate planning, will preparation, power of attorney, eldercare planning, resume writing, health benefits, and career coaching. The topics presented above were needed by the early retiree in retirement because they often reported preparation or comments about topics in the interviews.

In continuation of the research question compared to the conceptual framework, the results below will discuss the needs of the early retiree in relationship to the conceptual framework. The results were transferred in to participant composite tables for each of the interview questions. Therefore, Section 2 of this paper tells the early retirees' preretirement and retirement story further.

The first section related to the conceptual framework is the informational discussion about financial planning or wealth. The early retirees reported needing to plan for this topic and it was a topic presented in preretirement training and counseling.

The conceptual framework of this study combined the topics of lifeplanning and wellness to create a holistic snapshot of the early retiree in preretirement planning and preparation. The composite tables of the participants are located in the appendix, and paragraph summarizes are listed below.

The themes of Jim's retirement story reveal the need for various lifestyle changes within retirement. In his retirement role, Jim pursued a second career in college teaching through obtaining a masters degree in human resources. Jim revealed the emotional dynamics he experienced in retirement. He discussed the changes in relationships and the important conversations with significant others to maintain a successful transition into retirement. The planning for healthy life-styles through exercise and nutrition was vital to Jim's early retirement plan. At the core of Jim's planning for early retirement was financial planning and the details to maintain a stable income to support a positive lifestyle in retirement. Jim was challenged with the work role changes from one of high power in an executive position to the bottom of the ladder as an adjunct professor. In this shift, his self esteem varied and it created interesting conversations with significant others. He is still striving to make contributions to the community and re-establish his new world of work.

The themes of planning for Roy, besides financial preparation, included a focus upon work following his retirement. Roy took foreign language classes before retirement to prepare for teaching overseas after he retired. Roy planned many aspects of his life, including the creation of a social club with other retired men. A main focus in Roy's life was upon his family where he invested in his rela-tionships through the participation in a retreat for his immediate family. Roy admitted to the feelings of loss in retirement and spoke of the adjustment of roles within his family. Roy needed to create social networks to stay happy within retirement. The networks have served as social support for his experience in retirement. He also needed to remain intellectually engaged and prepared for other employment before retiring.

Within Steve's experience of retirement, the planning included many of the topics listed in the conceptual framework. Steve's focal point for retirement was upon the planning for his family. His wife had a job in the area and his daughters were preparing to enter college. Steve made significant decisions about geography in retirement based on family needs even though he would prefer a better cli-mate. In planning for retirement Steve did focus upon the preparation for a sec-ond career but regrets not pursuing further education for a teaching certificate. He currently teaches as an adjunct professor for a few colleges. He also wished he took more advantage of his military contacts and networking to assist in his tran-sition into retirement. Within the realm of physical fitness, Steve did participate in a physical as he retired and now uses that information as a baseline for his health and fitness. Steve needed to create a plan for social networks and support in retirement.

Bill reported, in his experience of retirement planning and the experience of retirement, a significant focus upon learning about finances. Bill experienced a major shift in companionship and relationships within retirement. He traveled significantly within his most recent work so when he retired he had to develop new friendships that were in the local area and not associated with work. He hinted of a self-esteem shift as fewer people contacted him and he had more time in his schedule. In regard to physical health, Bill participated in a physical at the age of 50 and changed his lifestyle according to the physician's recommendations. Although he did not plan to move immediately after retirement, he is now in the process of relocating to be closer to his family and grandchildren.

John's experience of retirement planning changed for this was his second retirement. He stated he disliked retirement so much the first time, he returned to another full-time job to escape retirement. John reported he planned much better for this retirement compared to the first one. He found the area of emotional awareness was challenging in retirement through dealing with issues of self-esteem and changes in relationships. For John, intellectual stimulation was very important and pursued a master's degree to pursue adjunct college teaching in retirement. In retrospect, John would have paid more attention to some of the areas discussed in this study as his preparation for retirement. John needed to focus further on a holistic aspect of life in retirement to be happier.

Summary of the Male Issues in Retirement

The discussions with the male participants in this study revealed a strong experience with relationships and emotional shifts in retirement. Many of the participants reported a shift in self-esteem, loss, and power as they transitioned into retirement. The focus was more on the relationship dynamics versus the change in financial status.

All of the males reported a need to further their education and prepare for second career experiences. Some of the males returned to school for masters degrees where others reported taking classes to assist in second careers. The need for intellectual stimulation was critical in the experience of retirement.

Three males reported participating in volunteer work while in retirement. The goal behind the volunteer work and the teaching was a way that the individual could give back to society. This appeared to be important to pass on knowledge and expertise to the younger generations.

Three of the males in this study reported a change in physical activity and nutrition. However, this did occur before they retired. As a perk in the organization, the executives were asked to participate in physicals. From the physicals, the participants reported changes in fitness and nutritional behavior.

A majority of the participants reported a greater focus upon family in retirement. Major decisions about geography and relationships were made based upon family issues in preparation and within the experience of retirement. Perhaps the males felt a need to make up for lost time that was created by their career involvement.

The first female participant was Mary and she participated in many various planning processes as she prepared for retirement. The most common theme for Mary was building and maintaining relationships with her husband and friends. She planned activities with her husband and friends to transition into retirement. Additionally, she looked at her and her husband's health in regards to physical activity and nutrition. She has planned and implemented new healthy eating habits and exercise. Mary reported retirement caused dramatic soul searching and a readjustment of her own identity. She even trained and became a foster parent as she retired as she wanted to contribute to others.

Cathy's experience of retirement follows the traditional model of retirement where the individual relocates to a warmer climate and no longer considers working. Cathy and her husband are building a new home in Atlanta to relocate closer to her daughter and grandchildren. She is also traditional in the sense of the complete reliance on her husband for planning retirement. Although she says she has not really planned for retirement, the interview revealed many comments about purchasing bikes for retirement and participating in classes at the local colleges.

Marlene's experience of retirement revealed a desire to pursue her life work through completing a higher level of academic degree to make a difference and help others. In her pursuit for higher learning, she developed her own wellness business that includes offerings of yoga classes, nutrition counseling, and reiki training. She also offers seminars on her topics of expertise. She is much more physically active in retirement and has continued her relationships through email and the cell phone. Marlene has been thinking about how she can make a difference to others through writing and hopes to increase her level of journaling.

Janice pursued retirement to experience things she really loved. She called it a pursuit for personal happiness. In Janice's planning for retirement, she prepared financially for the last 7–8 years, then moved to a new house and fixed it up before retirement. Janice is an avid gardener and enjoys painting and playing the piano. She has financially planned to be completely retired for about 2 years. Then she will return to the world of work but in a much lesser capacity as before. Janice is involved in learning in retirement but mainly in the area of art and stained glass.

Anna's retirement experience focuses around the emotional component of assisting her daughter to raise her grandchildren. She was frustrated by the lack of her organization's ability to create a flexible schedule for her needs forcing her to retire. Anna also travels extensively with her friends and is always looking for a new adventure. This is her time for intellectual growth as she plans for the next trip. She values her family and prayed hard to decide whether to retire or not. Anna does not regret her decision and loves her experience in retirement.

Summary of the Female Issues in Retirement

The female responses reveal a holistic response to planning for retirement specifically in the area of maintaining and developing important relationships. All of the women in this study did participate in learning following retirement through college classes, art classes or planning travel. Many of the women did not speak extensively on the topic of finances. In some situations, the financial perspective was or would be handled by the participants' husband. The women did plan for financial aspects of retirement but the conversation focused upon fulfilling a life mission to take care of self or taking care of family.

The women of the study were not as occupationally focused as the men in the study. One woman did continue on for further information to make a career change. However, most of the women did not focus on occupational aspects but on family and relationships.

Summary of Research Question 2

The table below represents the composite of all the participants in this stustudy. The topics of wellness and lifeplanning are supported in the planning and experience in retirement. The participants responded in various ways indicating whether they did plan, needed more planning or did not view the topic as important for planning in retirement. The participants revealed a need for planning in many of the lifeplanning and wellness topics.

Table 3
Wellness and Lifeplanning Concepts.

	Wealth	Geography	Companionship	Physical Fitness / Nutrition	Emotional	Intellectual	Occupational	Spiritual
Jim	X	X		X	X	X	X	
Roy	X	X	X	X	X	X	X	
Steve	X	X	X	X		X	X	X
Bill	X	X		X	X	X	X	
John	X					X	X	
Mary	X	X	X	X	X	X	X	X
Cathy		X		X		X		
Marlene	X	X		X		X	X	X
Janice	X	X		X	X	X	X	X
Anna	X	X			X	X		X

Table 3 reveals the participants' perspective and experience in planning for retirement balanced upon the lifeplanning and wellness model, a holistic model of the person and life. The participants' greatest planning needs were in the areas of intellectual stimulation, wealth creation and maintenance, geographical planning, and occupational and physical health. The topics reveal a holistic planning perspective for retirement.

As noted, all participants reported working or attending classes in retirement supporting the need for intellectual stimulation in retirement. It appeared to be a priority with the participant of this study. The participants were engaged in learning for college credit or for simple enjoyment.

The majority of the participants of this study considered their lifestyle with regard to their residence location. A few discussed the priority of moving closer to family and placing geographical concerns combined with family relationships. Other participants wanted to stay within their current community but reported discussions with significant people in their life to make this decision.

Wealth creation and maintenance was a priority for the participants in this study. Most of the participants planned for many years in the area of finances to allow for an early retirement. They created strategies and plans with private financial planners with little use of the organizational resources. The accumulation of wealth to support retirement allowed for the participant to pursue personal life interests without worrying about money in retirement.

Although some participants reported involvement with physical fitness before retirement, a majority of the participants were active or needed more participation in physical fitness within retirement. Some of the decisions with the men in this study were determined by physicals and meeting with physicians on the topic of health. The men used the retirement or executive physical as a motivator and guide to further physical fitness goals and involvement.

Another layer of concern for participants in this study was pertaining to occupational planning and second careers in retirement. Eight of the 10 participants reported working for money following retirement in various types of positions. Most acquired part-time and consulting work in different career fields compared to their career jobs. Some participants did return to college to receive higher levels of degrees to enter specific career fields.

The topic of emotional awareness was discussed by several participants through either preparing for retirement or being surprised by the emotional dynamic of retirement. Participants discussed the experience of change in relationships and emotions. Many wished they were able to plan for the emotional shock of retirement and better prepare for the changes in relationships. They wished for a specific awareness level before entering retirement. Many explored who they truly are after dismissing the work role they have held for many years.

One topic that lacked comments was companionship. However, the questions about companionship appeared to be discussed further within the topics of emotional awareness and control. All of the participants discussed the topic of relationships and changes in relationships within retirement. Therefore, the two topics could have been overlapped as a question. Therefore, this table misrepresents the importance of companionship in retirement.

The topic of spirituality was only supported by half of the participants. This could have occurred based upon the varying definitions between spirituality and religion. Some of the participants discussed the topic as participation in religious organizations while others described spirituality as personal happiness and pursuing a life mission. The women of the study had more responses and answers pertaining to spirituality in retirement compared to the men. A further clarification of the questions on this topic would provide a clearer understanding of spirituality in retirement.

The topics, as displayed above, were at various levels of need based upon how often individuals mentioned the topic. These topics were often not presented in the preretirement training programs offered to the early retirees in this study. Since these topics of preretirement training were not offered by the early retirees' organization, the question's component of satisfaction of the programs remains inconclusive.

In conclusion, more than half of the participants supported the lifeplanning and wellness concepts in the following areas: wealth, geography, physical fitness/ nutrition, emotional awareness/control, intellectual, occupational and spiritual. The only area not supported by at least half of the participants was the topic of companionship. However, this topic could be questioned because the majority of discussion on companionship occurred within the questions of emotional awareness and control. All of the participants reported responses reported experiences with the wellness and lifeplanning topics in retirement supporting a majority of the conceptual framework of retirement. Again, the early retirees needed more information in preparation for retirement than what the human resource departments provided them in training.

Section 3: Recommendations for Retirement from the Early Retirees

Within this study, additional open-ended questions were asked to probe the early retirees further about planning, preparation, and needs for retirement. The answers to these questions further explore the story of the early retirees' experience of retirement and planning.

One open-ended question was, What led you to select the age you retired? The respondents answers varied from family commitments, job dissatisfaction, the lack of ability to get promoted, and personal health. These topics could be viewed as planning and preparation topics for retirement.

It appears in the participant's answers, the reasons to retire ranged from changes in the organization to family considerations. Underlying the reasons to retire suggest a theme of searching for a new meaning and purpose in life. The main focus was upon self-happiness and relationships.

Table 4
Additional Questions: What Led You to Select the Age You Retired?

Name of Participant	Led you to select the age you retired? AD Q1–Question 27
Jim	Burn out, loss of value in career, I did not care about what I was doing.
Roy	Bonus of $20,000 was an incentive. I wanted something more
Steve	Family considerations. My oldest daughter was to start college. We were overseas and I was uneasy. Another daughter was going to start college in 2 years. We needed to be back in the states. I also had gone far as possible for promotions in the Air Force.
Bill	30 years at Hewlett Packard, fully vested. Decided before any downsizing. There was a reorganization, I was offered a job I did not like and I did not want to deal with it.
John	Changes in company, job satisfaction, probably should have waited until 62. With the current economy I would have stayed. I lost so much money in the stock market I can't recoop it.
Mary	Level of stress, It was hard for me to stop doing bedside nursing and still teach hospital nursing. (It was a moral dilemma) It was very stressful and I could not do it.

Table 4
Additional Questions: What Led You to Select the Age You Retired? (Continued)

Name of Participant	Led you to select the age you retired? AD Q1–Question 27
Cathy	When my children and husband finished college. I did not need the extra income
Marlene	I knew about 1 year in the corporate world I knew it wasn't my life. I was used to the security, did not like the environment and it pushed me out. I stayed and it became a challenge. I was passionate about helping people heal and I could not do it without more school. I started to work at a health food store and started school.
Janice	Self happiness. I was working on a project for 3 years and I completed my commitment to them. It worked for the both of us. It was completion of the project and then there were others to carry the project following my departure.
Anna	My daughter had twins and wanted to work part time. I asked for a flexible schedule At work and they would not grant me the request.

Another open-ended question pertained to the activities the early retiree was participating in within retirement. The question directly asked, What are you doing in your retirement? Many of the participants did report working for pay and participating in volunteer work. Table 6 represents the activities of the early retirees in this study. The early retirees' responses could present additional areas for planning and preparation for retirement.

Table 5
Additional Question What Are You Doing in Retirement?

Name of Participant	What are you doing in your retirement? AD Q7–Question 33
Jim	Teaching at two schools (intellectual), selling and consulting (cash flow benefits) community volunteer (personal satisfaction) I will probably do this forever.
Roy	Now I am doing geneology, looking at new ways to make it more interesting with some of the past. I am also Professor Sunshine to the local schools where I teach the solar system as student assemblies.

Table 5
Additional Question What Are You Doing in Retirement? (Continued)

Name of Participant	What are you doing in your retirement? AD Q7–Question 33
Steve	Teaching and spending time with my family. It's a big thing. I have opportunities to travel and to go out to dinner.
Bill	Volunteer work, (Winchester Nursing Home, Marytown, Committees at St. Joes), playing golf 1–2 times per week
John	Teaching 2 classes at MCC, macroeconomics at Columbia. I am making the final arrangements for accounting seminars for a consulting company.
Mary	Planting, taking in foster children. Activities with my husband.
Cathy	Fun things. Time for friends. Taking care of the home, I love to cook. I eat out. I do what I want when I want to do it.
Marlene	I am busier than when I worked a 40 hr week. I am doing health consultations, yoga, reiki therapy and I am also teaching it.
Janice	Testing software for old job, drawing, painting, gardening, piano, going to the health club, dinner with friends, some traveling, working on projects around the house.
Anna	Working part time at Jewel. Paying bills. Watching my grandkids grow up. Travel. Social events with friends. Go out to dinner. Went to Branson for a weekend. With ladies joined the theater club at Drury Lane. Go out for lunch. It is what I enjoy.

The information in this table reveal almost all of the participants have returned to work in retirement. A few have returned to work for their former organization as a consultant or trainer. Many are involved in volunteer work in the community and some have started second careers in a new field. Spending time with family also was a priority to the participants in this study. This further supports that retirees often do return to the workforce after retirement.

The last question the early retirees were asked in the study was about how they would coach another individual to retire. Table 6 presents the wisdom of the early retirees who participated in this study.

In Table 6, the participants reported preparation for retirement in many areas. The participants recommended to stay active and stay connected with friends.

The input from the retirees' revealed a wide range of planning needs for retirement. The bottom line of the retirees was to "enjoy yourself" in retirement.

Marlene stated in her final comments on retirement,

> Provide early on for financial needs. Make a will. Let funeral plans be known—organ donation—choose where you want to travel (maybe Elderhostel) and then ENJOY and live EVERY day! DO NOT just watch TV! Do NOT just baby-sit. Do NOT just go with seniors to places.Do yoga, read with young children, go to school and learn about alternative (natural) remedies so you are NOT dependent on doctors and prescriptions. Smile—laugh—find 5 things for which to be grateful EVERY day.

Marlene's perspective suggests living life and exploring every day, whereas, Anna's focuses upon the perspectives of living and enjoying life.

Table 6
The Wisdom of the Early Retirees.

Name of Participant	How would you coach others to retire?
Jim	#1 plan for it before the time comes–don't wait to the last minute–give time. #2 Don't do planning by yourself. Bring family in the process. Have a financial advisor you can trust and a physician. #3 From the advice of others–it is a very traumatic event–no man is an island–everything changes.
Roy	In business, it is great to do what you can do with what money can do. In academia, make sure you don't retire before you want to. Teaching is better than retiring. Teaching while retired is ideal.
Steve	Try to get skills up, whatever is lacking, such as computer skills. Get them up to speed before you retire. Financial questions, get those answered before you retire. Make a strong assessment of what you want to do—don't kid yourself. Plan accordingly. Don't take first job offer. Don't panic about sitting at home—go for a match. Use your contacts. Skills count but get your foot in the door through networking.
Bill	Have a plan to keep yourself busy (hobbies, volunteer work, part time work)

Table 6
The Wisdom of the Early Retirees. (Continued)

Name of Participant	How would you coach others to retire?
John	Plan early, review often. Know Self and Spouse. Get personal guidance in all areas—have the conversations with the right people. (table continues)
Mary	1. Make are sure about their benefits. 2. Have social ties and have people to do things with. It's important at our age.
Cathy	1. Have a plan to stay active and see people 2. Have money to do a few things you want 3. Have a good time 4. Don't worry
Marlene	Retire is just a word. It's another part of your life—Now you have time to learn something new—to take those walks—to connect with old friends. In other words, to fill a day with JOY—maybe volunteer—go to sleep every night knowing you had a GREAT day!
Janice	It's a self decision where the person should be emotionally, mentally, and financially prepared to do it. I don't know how you can go wrong. It's such a personal decision…When you have enough money or have another job to go to.
Anna	One door closes and another one opens. If it is time to retire, enjoy yourself Some people want to retire at 70 and you don't know you are going to live that long.

Anna's final statements on retirement follow,

> When it happened, you go through change. I don't have to wake up at 6 am anymore. I will never be rich but no one is going to tell me what to do. If you have money, go on a trip. As you grow older you think about what is important to you. Get up in the morning and say Thank you God. Go to bed and say thank you and hope you live until tomorrow. God wants to know if you did something good while you were here.

The suggestions of the early retirees imply a combination of the conceptual framework of lifeplanning and wellness concepts as a means for planning for retirement.

Summary

The purpose of the study was to explore the process and outcomes of the early retiree in preretirement planning. The early retirees of this study reported limited preretirement training programs were offered by their human resource departments. The retirees reported a strong need for a variety of topics and more comprehensive preparation for retirement. Therefore, the preretirement planning needs of the early retirees did not match the offerings of the human resource departments of their organizations. The foundation for retirement remains in the financial and health arena but additional topics and planning occurred in the transition to retirement. Within the conversations with the early retirees, there is still a consideration of who exactly would provide the training on these various topics. The study presents several topics for further investigation in the early retirement planning process.

Section 3:
The New Retirement

7

The Holistic Retirement

This study investigated preretirement training and the planning of 10 early retirees within the Chicago area to explore the need for further study of this topic and to suggest to organizations of the needs of early retirees heading into retirement. The study was conducted by interviews with 10 early retirees who have been retired for more than one year. The results of the study appear to suggest a holistic, life planning approach prior to retirement was needed for transition into retirement. The sections below will further discuss the outcomes of the study.

Research Question 1

What were the content topics of preretirement training and counseling offered by the early retirees' human resource department? Various content areas were provided in preretirement training at various levels of coverage as reported by the early retirees. The highest frequency of preretirement training topics reported were financial planning and health benefits. These two topics present the primary needs of the individual for survival in the transition into retirement. Human resource departments of the early retirees' studied are providing the content areas for basic information about pensions and benefits in retirement at infrequent levels.

Preretirement training has been an employee service and not mandated by the government (Ivancevich, 2001). The Employment Retirement Income Security Act (ERISA) of 1974 was created to ensure employees under private pensions received the benefits promised but it does not require an employer to provide a private pension (Ivancevich, 2001). There appears to be a lack of clarity in ERISA for providing preretirement training and information. ERISA states the organization must communicate to the employees the information about eligibility and disbursement for pension programs but there is no clear guidelines to how the information is to be provided. As the early retirees in this study stated, some received training while others received packets and booklets. To be in compliance with ERISA, businesses must provide detailed retirement benefit plan information to employees (Illinois Benefit Law, 2003). The descriptions of plan information must be provided to participants and beneficiaries in writing that is readable for an average participant to understand (Hall, 1999). The organizational difficulty of presenting preretirement training appears to be in the possible misrepresentation and legal ramification for providing incorrect retirement benefit information. Most participants in this study reported receiving financial and health benefit information; the impact of transitional assistance into retirement from the information depends upon the depth of information provided. A few other topics were presented, such as will preparation, estate planning, power of attorney, eldercare planning, resume writing, and career coaching, in preretirement training but it was to less than 5 of the participants. Essentially, the interviews indicate that companies are providing what they are required to provide and little more of what is legally required of human resource departments.

The investigation revealed a greater need for preretirement information on all of the concepts probed. Although the government does not require organizations to offer preretirement training, the early retirees were in great need of further information on the topics of inquiry: financial, estate planning, will preparation, power of attorney, eldercare planning, resume writing, health benefits, technology and computers, and career coaching. The majority of the participants only received information about finances and a little about health benefits.

This study appears to suggest that preretirement training has been ignored in some organizations, especially for early retirees. With the projected increase in early retirements (Drucker, 1999), organizations may be surprised with unexpected turnovers and the loss of key organizational leadership through unplanned early retirements. This could be prevented through offering preretirement training for retirement careers, job restructuring, and consulting within their current organization. From the data, human resource departments could devise comprehensive preretirement training programs that included all of the topics that were investigated.

Research Question 2

The second research question explored the areas the early retirees planned for before and during the transition into retirement. The second research question was not directly answered due to the way the study was conducted. The question did reveal the following content areas the early retirees viewed as important to the retirement transition process:

- Wealth–financial planning and security.

- Intellectual pursuits–intellectual engagement with tasks in retirement.

- Geography–decision making for the right place to live in retirement.

- Health and Physical–obtaining health benefits and care of one's physical well being.

- Emotional Awareness/Emotional Control–relationships with others and redefining roles in life.

- Occupational Pursuits–second careers and part-time employment.

- Spiritual Engagement—pursuit of one's happiness and relationships with God.

- Companionship—maintaining relationships and social support.

Table 3 in chapter 4 summarizes this data. The thread that connects these areas is a greater sense of care for oneself and in relationships with others. Perhaps the preretirement decision includes the pursuit of heartier relationships and a stronger commitment to lead a healthier lifestyle. It also may show a desire to pursue other life goals, experience different roles, and find a purposeful meaning in life. These ideas lead to the underlying assumption that early retirees are ready to reinvent their lives on their own terms, instead of the organizations'. In comparing the two research questions in order to answer question 3, training provided to early retiree by the human resource departments and the needs of the early retiree in retirement do not match as far as the transition process into retirement. The reinvention of identity that occurs within retirement needs further training and planning compared to what is offered by the human resource department.

Revisiting the Conceptual Framework of the Study

One segment of the conceptual framework of the study was built upon Lindahl's 1947 study revealing the communication gap of what managers thought employees wanted from work compared to the actual wants of the employees. The present study revealed a gap between what the early retirees received from the human resource department for preretirement preparation compared to what the early retirees' actually needed for transition into retirement. With this information, human resource departments can further understand the needs of the older employee and their potential personal and career planning needs in the future. This could assist in staff and succession planning for the organization. It could assist with the motivation and incentives offered to older employees as they prepare and plan for retirement or seek out employment after retirement. The study allows organizations to assess the potential ideas of employee retention and utilization of the early retirees following retirement.

The second segment of the conceptual framework of the study was built upon combining lifeplanning and wellness concepts as a topic suggestion guide for preretirement planning and the preparation process as listed in the prior section. This section will further describe the concepts related to the insights from the participants of the study.

Wealth

The participants of the study reported wealth and financial planning as the top priority of preparation for retirement. The ability to stabilize and project finances to leave a position and retire was a key factor to having the ability to retire. Many of the participants reported planning early and diversifying their portfolio to achieve the ability to retire when they had planned. Many spoke of spending years of time with financial planners while others took on learning all they could about finances to have a comfortable retirement. Some did report a financial need to return to work in retirement due to the stock market collapse within the past few years. Within preretirement planning, the early retiree needed information from organizational and independent sources. The early retirees also stated the financial process needed to start very early within an individual's career.

Intellectual Pursuits

The participants of the study reported an extensive need for information and planning for intellectual pursuits. Three of the participants reported returning to formal schooling to receive advanced degrees to further their own intellectual pursuits. All of the participants reported participation in learning experiences through travel, formal schooling, or hobby-related learning. The participants reported attending local colleges and universities to acquire additional college degrees. Other reported participation in art classes and other classes for enjoyment at the local community colleges. The comments suggest a planning and preparation need for the transition into retirement. The preparation for intellectual stimulation was necessary for these individuals. As learning in retirement programs are expanding at many United States colleges and universities (Garydn, 2000), retirees are becoming more involved in lifelong learning (Eisen, 1998). Perhaps, this could indicate a need for further career development processes in organizations for the early retirees that departed for second careers.

Geography

The foundation for the geographical planning for the early retirees was generally based upon the location of family members. Although many of the participants reported remaining where they were located at the current time, the decisions were based upon the current location of significant family members with the desire to remain in close proximity. One participant reported that when her husband retires, they will relocate to Atlanta to be closer to their children and grandchildren. The geographical decision rested upon employment opportunities and family commitments.

Health

The participants of this study did report a priority of caring for health within retirement. The first topic of most importance was the discussion of obtaining adequate health benefits either through their former employer or independently. Three of the participants reported obtaining adequate health benefits has continued to be a struggle within retirement. It appeared several organizations did not offer health benefit plans to the early retiree. Most reported finding adequate health benefits independently. This issue could impact the Medicare system in the years to come through the projected overload of participants drawing from the system when the baby boomers retire, in approximately 10 years, and there might not be enough money to support these people (Poulos, 1997).

In addition to the discussion of health benefits, the topics of physical fitness and nutrition were addressed in the interviews. Although it was an important topic for planning and maintaining in retirement, many of the participants had made healthy lifestyle changes prior to retirement. The discussion of concern for physical well being supports the above stated increase of care for self that appears to occur in retirement. The retirees appear to be searching for a more enjoyable life by retiring and to have that experience they are clear about taking care of their health and physical well being.

Emotional Awareness/Emotional Control

A sense of loss appears to occur within the transition to retirement with changes in relationships and roles. Large contributions to the workplace and work roles sometimes cause sacrifices in the ability to spend time with family. Through this the individual might feel a bit cheated out of life. After all, being in the provider role has placed great stress on family relationships, commitments and friendships all to keep the house going and money coming in. There appears to be a sense of regret within some of the early retirees conversations and an interest in regaining what they had lost through all the commitment to work. The time spent in retirement is to make up for perceived missed opportunities due to work commitments. It is a time to make up for lost time in retirement. In retirement, the early retiree has the opportunity to explore and really discover what is truly going on within the family. For some participants, discussions occurred with all of the family members to prepare for the changes in the role of retirement. A few of the participants reported a greater time commitment to family and an expanding of relationships.

Interpersonal relationships with family and friends became a priority in retirement. Several participants discussed their relationship with their significant other and family members as a priority for success in retirement. It appeared many relied on coworkers' friendships during their career years that dissolved when the individual retired. Some early retirees stated a need work on building new networks and associations of friends. The emotional dynamic supports the need for additional companionship within retirement. The early retirees discussed the loss of coworker friends and the need to develop new friendships in retirement.

Occupational Pursuits

Several of the participants in this study started second careers and returned to work following retirement. The second career participants matched academic endeavors to occupational pursuits. One participant reported a stronger need for technological training before retirement. He stated his lack of technology skills has hindered his ability to enter into specific career fields and limited his earning potential. Older adults sometimes need to be retrained in computer skills to return to the workforce (Czaja, 2001; Poulos, 1997). The discussion of the need for computer training prior to retirement could assist in the retirees' retirement career options. Several of the participants that did return to work obtained mentors in the field to assist with the transition into the second career fields. These mentors were often obtained through academic institutions and community volunteerism.

Spiritual Engagement

The participants of the study did report a spiritual component of the retirement process. Many said it was a continuation of their current beliefs but others wished they had spent more time thinking and planning in this area. Some participants reported an experience of self change with a pursuit for self happiness during the conversation of spirituality in retirement. The participants stated a purpose and new meaning in life emerged as they entered retirement. A common theme of contribution and service arose within several of the participants whether it was serving the community or working within the foster care system. The importance of service is promoted in several spiritual settings and a piece of the puzzle of retirement.

Companionship

The relationships within retirement are vital to a positive retirement experience. The participants of this study expressed the need for conversations to occur within significant relationships. The participants also discussed the relationship and connection to old work friends. One participant reported as he transitioned into retirement his phone started ringing less and he felt others no longer thought it was important to call him. He found out those friends no longer needed him. Work relationships are often proximity based, based only on location, and therefore when an individual retires the need for the friendship no longer exists. Therefore, the validation of a lot of friends, based on work alone, was an illusion to the possibility of the friendships that will remain during retirement. Many of the respondents did report missing work colleagues and a sudden lack of friends. This appears to suggest the thinking and planning for the creation of social networks and affiliation long before an individual enters retirement. The respondents did discuss the variation of maintaining friends and established networks that started before retirement.

The summary suggests a holistic model for retirement preparation is needed. This will be vital as the Baby Boomer Generation enters retirement.

8

Retirement in Transition

The Retirement Transition

The retirement transition is a topic with many dimensions to further explore and understand. Several transitions occur for the early retiree and the important people in the early retiree's life. This next section discusses briefly a few areas of interest for the retirement transition.

Reinvention of Identity in Retirement

All of the participants in the study reported their experience of transition into retirement. This was most evident in the change of work roles and roles within the family. The results indicated that participants were involved in dramatic soul searching and transformation. Others experienced the process of loss, grieving and rebuilding of identity following retirement. The individuals appeared to seek out new environments to further define who they were now that they were retired and establish a new mission and purpose in life.

The Care of the Self in Retirement

The participants of this study did report an interest in healthy behaviors while in retirement. A few of the participants reported completing physical examinations to create a baseline for further health planning. A few participants did report more attention was paid to physical fitness and nutrition following the physicals. One participant suggested to others to include a family physician in the retirement planning phase for guide and maintain good health conditions in retirement.

Friendships and support systems were important as reported by the participants in the study. One participant created a retired male coffee group to meet each Tuesday morning. The majority of the participants discussed looking to support from their family and friends as they transitioned into retirement. Many had conversations to discuss the movement and changes as entering retirement. Several mentioned that more conversations were needed to help the transition.

Life Mission in Retirement

As one of the participants mentioned before, entering retirement caused dramatic soul searching. Other participants reported the loss of status and clout. There appeared to be a loss of a sense of mission initially as the individual entered retirement. Some of the participants reported a strong attachment to work roles that were released as they entered retirement. Two participants did report a clear mission in retirement where they were going to continue in the field of teaching in other settings and the other discussed a commitment to family and her grandchildren.

Evidently, a conversation of exploration could occur regarding the topic of an individual's life mission. Would the transition process become easier if an individual explored their life mission before entering retirement? One participant reported retiring twice and expressed the problems he experienced in his first retirement. He felt he lacked vision and did not understand what the retirement experience would be for him. He also stated his family and personal relationships were in great conflict, due to his retirement, and he felt lost. This example appears to display how the lack of planning for retirement can be a difficult experience. This participant did return to work full time and then recently retired again with a better plan.

Transforming Retirement

There is a transformation on the horizon for retirement (Dychtwald, 1999; Stein, 2000). Therefore, the interpretation of the data is linked to other subject areas. The subject areas are of potential consideration for the decision making for preretirement training and a further understanding of early retirement. This section discusses several ideas about retirement related to other subject areas and present ideas for future exploration.

Comparing Retirement to Fowler's Stages of Faith

In Fowler's stages of faith, the third stage is where a person is locked into following the rules and confirms to the norms of society. It is important to be working and be a contributor to society. When an individual gives up the work role, what is there value to society? The conflict occurs through societal norms of remaining in the workforce viewed in a more positive light compared to retiring. If the retiree decides to volunteer and contributes to society, the retiree would fit Fowler's life stages where an individual moves in to the category of a life of service. This could be reflected in the retirees that spoke about contribution to children, taking in foster children and grandchildren. The experience of volunteerism in retirement also matches the concept of Erikson's (1982) generativity, where the retirees continues to build the society through passing on knowledge and developing others to follow in their footsteps. The participants in this study expressed service as an activity in retirement.

Maslow's Hierarchy in Retirement

The early retirees do not need to climb the corporate ladder any longer. However, what are the needs of the early retiree with respect to Maslow's hierarchy of needs? The categories of the hierarchy of needs included the topics of physiological, safety, social, esteem, and self-actualization needs. The early retirees appeared to be concerned with the physiological needs, regarding money matching Maslow's basic concepts of needs. Then another layer of concern for the early retiree was their own self-esteem, regarding who am I to others, and social needs with friends and family. The males reported changes in self esteem and self worth entering retirement. One participant stated that his level of perceived importance appeared to be reduced when he retired. The females did not discuss changes in self-esteem and self-worth because of the work to retirement change. Finally, the early retiree was concerned about their mission in life an reaching self-actualization. Even in retirement, the participants did not feel completely at the self-actualization level in life. A few discussed the losses of power and prestige in retirement. Other discussed the changes in relationships and friendships. There appeared to be a striving for finding purpose and being empowered within oneself again within retirement. A study could be conducted with early retirees and needs relating to Maslow's hierarchy of needs. Perhaps the study could uncover the need structure for early retirees compared to other younger in the life cycle.

The study could also be balanced on the hierarchy of needs and career development. It might uncover the motivation for early retirement.

Midlife Crisis

The early retirees wanted more from life than what their current work was offering them. Some reported feeling cheated from family and personal interests while working. Perhaps, the increase in early retirements could be connected to the term of "midlife crisis" where an individual is seeking new meaning and purpose in life. Often it is a time where the individual asks, is this all there is to life (Sheehy, 1995)? As the individual entering midlife explores this topic, they might decide retirement is the best option for living out the remainder of their life in the most amount of happiness and time to enjoy important people in their lives.

Frankl and Motivation

Human beings' quest for understanding the meaning in life could also be driving the increase in early retirement. The internal struggle of what is the purpose of life compared to how life is being lived could cause some of the struggles in the transition into retirement. Frankl (1992) spoke of his experiences in a concentration camp and moving through difficult experiences while maintaining a solid internal locus of control and positive reflection toward life. The participants in this study were redefining their life mission, purpose and roles.

Sheehy's Middlescence

Sheehy (1995) discussed the topic of middlescence, where an individual in midlife experiences a second adolescence. Perhaps, the concept of middlescence could be renamed to reflect a definition that adds the service and contribution. The possibility of a new definition of retirement could include the idea of returning to youthful play combined with service and contribution to pass on to the generations behind. A term of renewal might be a better fit for the experience of revisiting joys of earlier life and guiding the future.

Support for Hope Meadows

As discussed earlier, the concept of intergenerational mentoring was presented through the example of Hope Meadows, a community with a foster grandparent system. This concept appears to be supported in this study with the interest of several participants that have been involved in volunteer work, teaching and foster parenting. Through the concepts of generativity presented by Eriskon (1982), there continues to be motivation to assist others grow into society. Perhaps, the research could be revisited to explore the concepts of generativity and the early retiree.

An Exploration of Erikson's Geotranscendence

Erikson (1982) presented the concepts of geotranscendence in his lifecycle literature as the experience of complete happiness and acceptance of one's life. The participants of this study were happy with their decision to retire early and expressed quite frequently a general happiness with the life they have created in retirement. The experience of geotranscendence could be explored and potentially challenged for the possibility of this experience happening earlier than Erikson may have predicted. Perhaps, it could change the ages of the life cycle.

Changes of the Life Cycle

This study of early retirees could impact the stereotypical age requirements for retirement. Might the life cycle theorists benefit from a revision of the actual age categories of the stage of retirement and create a new pattern for living? Perhaps, this study suggests a complete change in the life pattern where full time employment is only a small portion of an individual's life and the focus on an individual's live purpose comes to be a greater aspect. What if people did not follow the stereotypical pattern of the world of work and pursued their life mission and passion earlier in life? What would the world be like if individuals' tapped into leading from life mission instead of "what is right" and under the stereotypical rules of society?

How would the world be different if high school students tapped into their life mission at the start of their careers instead of at the end of their careers? Perhaps a study could be conducted on career development and the early retiree to discuss the options presented and the driving force of work for these individuals. The early retirees in the present study reported leaving their job because of the lack of interest in the work, inability for promotion and a feeling of no longer making a contribution. The exploration of early retirees leaving the workforce could assist organizations in succession planning and career planning. What do organizations need to offer employees to keep them in the organization?

Contributions to the Literature

This study suggests a revised model for comprehensive preretirement training as shown through the reported planning areas of the early retirees. With the above data, the study supports a holistic approach, combining general lifeplanning and wellness concepts, to achieve a successful transition into early retirement. The content topics that may be supported based upon this include financial planning, legal matter planning, health benefit planning, geographic planning, companionship planning, physical fitness and nutrition planning, emotional awareness and control planning, intellectual planning, occupational planning, and spiritual planning. This study expanded Beehr's (1986) model proposed planning for retirement as the individual expectations of retirement, the present state of the individual, health, finances, work life, and the pursuit of leisure interests.

Based on this conclusion, a proposed model for preretirement training and employee services is presented below. The model includes a combination of the human resource department sponsored topics already offered in limited preretirement training, lifeplanning concepts, and wellness concepts. The transition into retirement is complex. Upon completion of this study, the proposed model for a comprehensive preretirement training program or employee services is displayed below. The figure identifies human resource department compliance topics, under ERISA, granted the organization offered a pension plan and health benefits in retirement. The figure further designates the content areas to either work/life benefits or potential employee assistance program offerings. The figure suggests a holistic approach to preparation for retirement throughout the individual's career.

Initially, the life planning and wellness model included the following topics:

- Wealth.

- Intellectual Pursuits.

- Geography.

- Physical Health.

- Emotional Awareness/Emotional Control.

- Occupational Pursuits.

- Spiritual Engagement.

- Companionship.

This model was blended with the initially investigated preretirement training topics of financial, estate planning, will preparation, power of attorney, eldercare planning, resume writing, health benefits, technology and computers and career coaching to create the model presented below.

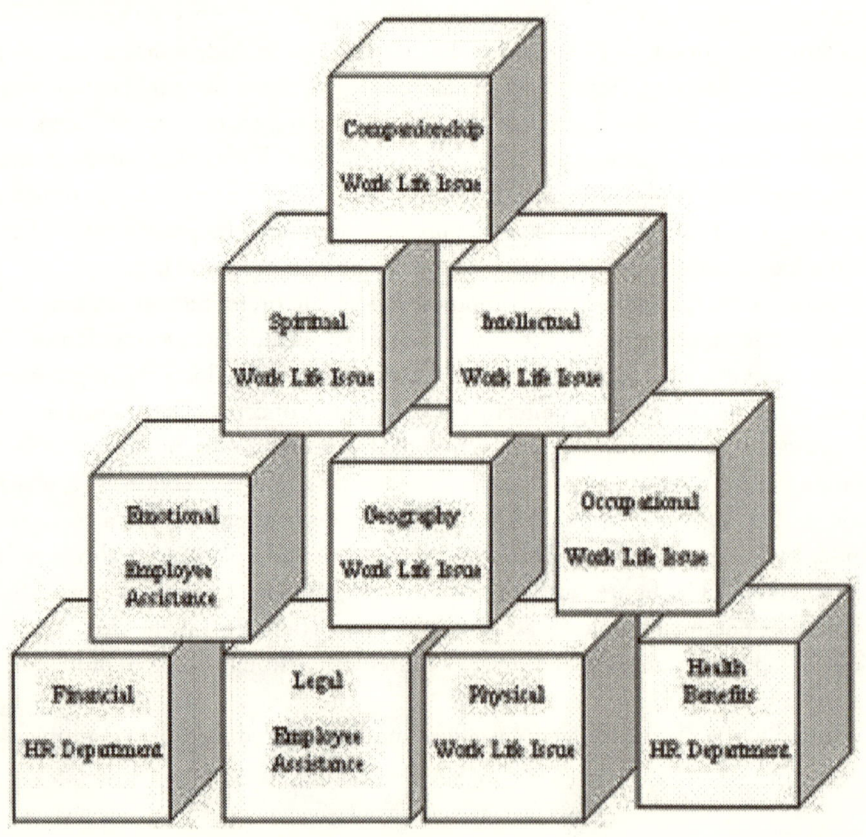

Figure 4. Building Blocks for Successful Retirement.

The model proposes options for human resource professionals to consider when determining benefit programs, work/life programs and employee assistance programs. The order of the blocks indicate that the blocks on the lower level must first be organized to move up to the other level blocks. For instance, the financial, legal, physical, and health aspects of retirement must be considered first before planning for the other categories. This is supported by the number of times the participants mentioned the topics as areas of preretirement training that were addressed by their human resource departments. The blocks above the bottom row are important areas to consider but are to be considered after the lower blocks are accomplished.

Further, the categories of human resource department, employee assistance and work/life issue present organizational structure ways to administer the topics. The human resource department categories of financial and health benefits link to possible compliance issues under ERISA. The employee assistance categories of emotional and legal are potential areas the human resource department may offer outside referrals or sources to assist the retiring individual. The work/life categories of physical, geography, occupational, spiritual, intellectual, and companionship are suggested as innovations for inclusion in an individual's career life and holistic benefits program. The model suggests a redesign of benefits and programs for individuals in planning for a smooth transition into retirement.

The proposed topics are only slightly changed from the original model designed by Hunter (1980), which included the topics of work, physical health, mental health, retirement income, financial planning, employment, consumer information, housing, social relationships, legal concerns, leisure time, widowhood, death and dying, and sexuality.

This study supports the existing research of retirement regarding continuity (Atchely, 1983), the cycle of leisure, learning and work (Stein, 2000), and preretirement training (Hunter, 1980). The early retirees did report in the experience of retirement the importance of setting a schedule and maintaining relationships with family, friends and work colleagues. The study did support the combination of phases of intellectual involvement through taking classes, involvement in travel and hobbies and periods of flexible employment. All of the participants supported the topic of preparation and planning for transitioning into retirement.

The redefinition of retirement presented by Dytchwald (1999) and Stein (2000) continue to be supported within this study. Throughout the study, it appeared the early retirees reported their contribution to society as they now had more time to make a difference. It is through this contribution the perception and stereotype of retirement is challenged. The old concepts of pure rest and relaxation in retirement are now in the past. The future lies with more opportunity for early retirees to express their true life mission in a variety of ways, through family contributions, volunteerism, mentoring, and teaching.

9

The Future Impact of the Boomers Retirement

In conversation with the participants, some asked what truly is the role of the human resource department as an individual is retiring. Is there a responsibility to the employee from the organization to provide more comprehensive preretirement training? The key aspect of the decision making for an organization to expand the offerings of preretirement training would depend on the return on investment to the organization. An organization could explore the option of a phase retirement plan where the organization offers the early retiree a half-time position and then hires a younger worker with the cost savings of a more tenured employee's reduced salary. Then, the early retiree could serve in a mentoring capacity to the younger worker. The majority of the early retirees reported returning to teach and share with others the knowledge and their experience with others. Guiding the future generations appeared to emerge in the discussions with the early retirees of this study.

Another cost-saving issue to explore would be the creation of a center for mentoring and coaching composed of early retirees. The early retirees could coach the young executives about the history and methods of the organization. The early retirees reported a need for continued intellectual stimulation and a feeling of a sense of loss of companionship with the loss of work relationships. The work of mentoring younger employees could assist meet the needs of the eager young employee and the early retirees' need for intellectual stimulation and companionship. Through the maintenance of organizational knowledge, through using the early retirees, there would be a lowered cost of training the new employees.

Further studies could be conducted to understand the depth of each of the topics presented for preretirement training. With a larger sample size, the depth and need of the content topics could be defined and explored. A shift in geographical location of the study, to a wider national sample, could reveal a United

States cultural composite of the important content topics for preretirement training.

A more in-depth study of the emotional aspects of the transition to retirement may be beneficial to the future retirees in the baby boomer population. Perhaps, the creation of a model for emotional awareness and relationship enhancement in the planning and implementation of retirement could reduce the stress of individuals entering retirement. A look at the identity transformation in retirement might provide organizations and families with powerful tools to support and utilize the individuals transitioning into retirement.

As this study has presented, the needs of early retirees' range in topic areas traditionally offered by organizations to other more personal, individual issues. Therefore, the human resource departments of organizations might consider exploring the topic of benefits to offer vouchers to acquire both the financial and emotional aspects of planning and experiencing retirement. Possibly, the component could be explored or added to the employee assistance programs that many organizations already support. The component of retirement preparation counseling could be explored through the benefit offerings of an employee assistance program.

The study revealed the early retirees' strong desire and involvement with intellectual pursuits entering the retirement phase of life. However, none of the organizations offered intellectual options in preparation for retirement. There were minimal offerings of computer and technology preparation or career coaching, where these topics were needed by early retirees. Therefore, an organization might explore a partnership with a local community college or university to offer lower tuition rates and/or tuition reimbursement. Some early retirees might not be technologically developed due to high positional rank within the organization. For instance, administrative staff may have managed the computer functions for the higher ranking individual thereby creating a need for technology training for the early retiree.

The study further supported a need to understand the decision making process for retirement. This study viewed the experience of early retirees and further studies could support the human resource succession planning process by creating an understanding of the early retiree's decision making process. The organization could be better prepared for early retirements and plan for the potential organizational loss from the retiring individual.

The transition process into retirement is an area worth further exploration. The participants of this study reported changes in identity, financial standing, status, relationships, and life patterns. Each of these items impacted their daily lives and the significant others in their life.

Testing New Models of Flexible Scheduling

As telecommuting and flextime is increasing in popularity, the human resource departments could start exploring varying work schedules. First the human resource departments could assess critical work needs and times, similar to the flex-time concept. Then the human resource departments could start testing with flexible work schedules to increase motivation and a greater balance in life and work. Perhaps, this could increase employee retention rates and test the models for promoting flexible work schedules to employees considering early retirement. The flexible work schedules would allow older workers to remain in the workforce and guide the younger employees with organizational knowledge and tradition.

When Should Retirement Planning Begin?

This is a question that could be further explored. Retirement appears to be a disconnection in life, an ending and a new beginning, so when might the planning begin? The consideration for including retirement in the career planning process from the start of a career could be the start of a smoother transition. Early conversations in relationships and the visualization of how retirement might look like could help the transition. The visualization process of a successful retirement could assist in the planning of the transition into retirement. Perhaps a dreaming of the process would guide the feelings and needs and wants while in retirement to drive the need for further planning.

Reinventing Work Life Benefits

As a benchmark for success, Starbucks has a unique set of benefit offerings for individuals who work more than 20 hours per week in their organization. The benefit package includes items important to the current times such as child care, adoption assistance, domestic partner benefits, and adult/elder care services. The essence of a work life program is presented in their segment called Working Solutions (http://www.starbucks.com/aboutus/SB-YSB-US-HR.pdf) where information resources and materials are available for other aspects of life outside of the workplace. This model supports a holistic view of the employee.

Implications for Change and Social Impact

Implication 1: Teaching and Mentoring

Several of the participants in the study reported a return to teaching or mentoring following early retirement. This may indicate a need for the creation of a teaching or mentoring program as a function of a training department in an organization. This could help prevent the loss of organizational knowledge as an early retiree departs and would support the organization. A program of this nature could support the need for the early retiree to keep intellectually engaged.

All of the participants in the study reported involvement with an academic or learning environment. Some participants reported returning for advanced degrees while others reported participation in local community college art classes or travel. This discussion further supports the continued existence and creation of learning in retirement programs for older adults. The retirees continue to be interested in learning and refining intellectual depth.

This issue presents the need for utilization and skills of the retirees within the organization. A strong mentoring program would empower the younger employees and support succession planning within the organization. This could transform organizational structure and career development within organization. Plus, it would reduce the loss of organizational culture and knowledge as more baby boomers head toward retirement. The loss of productivity created by the loss of organizational knowledge could be prevent through creating teaching and mentoring programs.

Implication 2: Working in Retirement

Several of the participants did return to a paying position after retirement. This suggests that early retirees do return to work following retirement. The implication of this pattern is for an organization's openness to recruit and hire older workers. The world of work could be challenged as the amount of actual workers reduces with the predicted mass retirements of the baby boomer generation (Costa, 1989). Therefore, the structure of work schedules and hiring could be revised in the future. Some of the early retirees that reported working also spoke about flexible schedules and working according to a self determined schedule. Organizations may need to change the current pattern of work schedules to include flexibility for the returning retired worker to the workforce.

The changes of organizational restructuring could impact the amount of workers in the workforce and potentially stabilize the predicted crash of the social security system. The organizations could then promote and hire additional older workers to support their organization and maintain productivity levels. Society might change their perception of older workers returning to the workforce and transform the perspective of working in retirement to one of acceptance and expectation.

Implication 3: Public Policy

Are organizations meeting the public policy requirements for benefit or training offerings in the area of retirement? Public policy makers could become concerned with the organizational responsibility to its employees with the pending collapse of social security and Medicare. Within this realm, is it the government's concern to enforce policy on organizations to better prepare retirees, especially with the projected baby boomer retirement?

Implication 4: Health Benefits

The participants reported difficulty in obtaining information and adequate coverage for health benefits within the study. With the health benefit challenge in mind, it might be beneficial for a review of public policies regarding access to health care for the retiree. As the baby boomer generation will head toward retirement, the need for the topic of adequate, affordable access to health care might be considered as an item under review for policy makers. The United States may obtain a great deal of knowledge if the policy makers were to review the system for health care with retirees in Sweden (Lassey & Lassey, 2001). Perhaps, a new prepay health care system could be created to support the future retirees similar to the college savings program of Upromise in addition to Medicare.

Implication 5: Civic Responsibility

Civic responsibility is a topic for consideration in relation to the increase in retirees in the United States culture. Many of the participants reported involvement in volunteer work, commitment to family, and teaching in retirement. It appears from these responses the participants could benefit from participation and contribution to younger members within the organization or organizational mentoring. One participant reported training and becoming a foster parent to teenaged children in her retirement. She felt her role as a mother never went away and it was an important contribution to society to become a foster parent. All of the participants reported the many ways they contribute to society during retirement.

Implication 6: New Career Models

This study suggests an exploration of career models. What is it that drives the individual to retire early? In this study, many of the early retirees reported the inability to move upward in the organization and a lack of interest in work as reasons for retirement. What could be added in the career cycle to keep individuals working? As the United States' baby boomers head toward retirement, how will the organizations keep running? What is necessary for retention strategies of the early retiree or the mid career employee? The discussion of new career models could be designed to incorporate a balance work and family life. The days of the huge commitment to work without time for family may be a career pattern of the past in order to retain committed employees. The resign of career models could address the midlife career and the transform the issue of retirement to end a career.

Implication 7: Preretirement Training

The preretirement training appeared to be limited and marginal, as reported by the participants in this study. Perhaps, the human resource department representatives could reevaluate the system of benefit planning, specifically preretirement training. The concept of lifeplanning and wellness could be combined to support a career planning component early in an individual's career to prepare throughout the career lifetime for retirement. The combination of concepts could lead to the initiative of work/life balanced career issues that would include the discussion of retirement.

Implication 8: Health Promotion

The study revealed the executives of the organizations were offered physical examinations at the age of 50. Following the examinations, a few of the participants reported changing dietary and fitness patterns that led to a healthier lifestyle. Other participants reported changes in diet and expanding physical fitness levels. The organization could create a healthier work environment, with healthier employees, if the organization could explore a partnership with a local hospital to offer physical examinations, stress tests, nutrition and wellness counseling as an employee benefit. Further, if the opportunity existed the organization could partner with the hospital sponsored health club, if available, to promote overall wellness in the organization. Some organizations already offer this benefit. This could be in addition to supporting healthy lifestyles of the individuals preparing for retirement.

Implication 9: Learning Communities

Local colleges and universities could assist in the transition process into retirement. The colleges and universities could create learning communities for the retirees in many categories to support the transition. The career centers at these institutions could support the retirement process through offering courses and learning communities on the topics of second careers, entrepreneurial skills, starting a business, and job searching. The psychology departments and counseling centers of these institutions could assist with programming on the topics of reinvention of identity in retirement, interpersonal relationships and building support networks. The institutions could create centers for retirement transition to support individuals entering retirement.

Implication 10: Redesigning Human Resource Departments and Benefits

Within the study of training and counseling for retirement, many of the participants were disappointed with what was offered by the human resource department. Offering preretirement training as an exclusive program, could be combined with a new, update work/life initiative that reviews the patterns of the life and career cycle that meets the needs of the individual today. A careful review of the lifecycle could reveal clearly the changing dynamics of an aging population and the changing career patterns of the baby boomer generation. Perhaps, the work life review could indicate and guide the reinvention of work life benefit programs for many organizations. Starbucks was mentioned above for being proactive and forward thinking in the realm of designing compensation and benefit packages to meet the needs of the current times.

Implication 11: Redesigning the Retirement Benefit

Within the interviews of this study, the participants reported receiving a combination of in house training and vouchers to receive the education to prepare for retirement. Perhaps, the best practice for human resource departments with limited resources would be to create an outlined guide of the suggested topics for preretirement training and then offer vouchers to obtain the information outside of the organization. Another way to redesign the benefits would be to combine the efforts within the employee assistance program offerings.

Summary

In summary, the process and experience of retirement is in transition. The old views of retirement are changing and being replaced with a new view of being retired. The newly retired view retirement as a time for learning, growth, fun, and contribution to family and the community. With the new view of retirement, the human resource offerings for preretirement training and counseling need to change. Organizations could benefit from the creation of an updated perspective on retirement and the contributions a retired employee could offer the organization.

Conclusion

The journey of preparation and transition into retirement is complex. We need to initiate candid conversations about retirement within our homes and workplaces to prepare for the future Boomers retirement. What rests at the core of the retirement discussion is the search for meaning in life, contributions to others and the unfolding of a specific life mission.

The future of this book relies on your efforts to transform the perception of retirement in society. The old paradigm of retirement is simply not valid in today's society. We need advocates to communicate the requests, desires and interests of Baby Boomers in their retirement years. The Baby Boomer generation has been responsible for transforming many aspects of American life, retirement will be the next challenge. I invite you to participate.

The New Retirement is emerging. As the Baby Boomers head toward retirement and the taboo truth about retirement is revealed, we as a society can become empowered to understand retirement and utilize retirees more effectively. The time and talent of many retirees are underutilized in today's society. We are at a critical turning point in families, organizations and as a society as the Baby Boomers retire. The future rests in our hands. Will you be a positive influence to society and advocate for the transformation of a New Retirement?

Together, we can create the best New Retirement ever!

With Regards, Doc Maria
—March 2004

References

Anderson, C. E., & Weber, J. A. (1993). Preretirement planning and perceptions of satisfaction among retirees. *Educational Gerontology, 19,* 397–406.

Atchley, R. (1983) *Aging, continuity and change.* Belmont, CA: Wadsworth.

Babbie, E. (1998). *The practice of social research.* Belmont, CA: Wadsworth.

Bahrami, B. (2001). Factors affecting faculty retirement decisions. *Social Science Journal, 38*(2), 297–306.

Baker, M. (2002). The retirement behavior of married couples: evidence from the spouse's allowance. *The Journal of Human Resources, 37*(1), 1–34.

Baltes, P., & Ulrich Mayer, K., Eds. (1999). *The Berlin Aging Study. Aging from 70 to 100.* Cambridge, UK: Cambridge University Press.

Beehr, T. (1986). The process of retirement: A review and recommendations for future investigation. *Personnel Psychology, 39,* 31–55.

Birren, J. (2000). Using the gift of long life: Psychological implications of the age revolution. In S. H. Qualls and N. Abeles (Eds.), *Psychology and the Aging Revolution. How We Adapt to Longer Life* (pp. 11–19). Washington, DC: American Psychological Association.

Bogdan, R., & Biklen S. (1998). *Qualitative research for education: An introduction to theory and methods.* Needham Heights, MA: Allyn & Bacon.

Bradley, S. K. (2002). Retirement dress rehearsal. *Journal of Financial Planning, 15*(1), 28–30.

Castellano, J. (2002). Restoring public confidence. *Journal of Accountancy, 193*(4), 37–41.

Cauldron, S. (2002). Retirement at risk: what HR must do. *Workforce, 81*(4), 28–32.

Charmaz, K. (2000) Grounded theory. Objectivist and constructivist methods. In N. Denzin & Y. Lincoln (Eds.), *TheHandbook of Qualitative Research* (pp. 509–535). Thousand Oaks, CA: Sage Publications.

Christians, C. G. (2000). Ethics and politics in qualitative research. In N. Denzin, & Y. Lincoln (Eds.), *The handbook of qualitative research.* (pp. 133–155) Thousand Oaks, CA: Sage Publications.

Colaizzi, P. (1978) Psychological research as the phenomenologist views it. In R. S. Valle & M. Kings (Eds.) *Existential-phenomenological Alternatives for Psychology.* (pp. 48–71). New York: Oxford University Press.

Corning, P. (1969). *The history of medicare.* Washington, DC: Social Security Administration.

Costa, D. (1998). *The evolution of retirement: an american economic history, 1880–1990.* Chicago: University of Chicago Press.

Creswell, J. (1994). *Research design. Qualitative and quantitative approaches.* Thousand Oaks, CA: Sage Publications.

Czaja, S. (2001). Technological change and the older worker. In J. Birren & K. W. Shaie (Eds.) *Handbook of the Psychology of Aging.* (pp. 547–568). San Diego, CA: Academic Press.

Dalton, D., Carins, D., et al. (1995). Human resource management and employee turnover and transfer: What we need to know is not always what we need. In G. Ferris, S. Rosen & D. Barnum (Eds.) *Handbook of Human Resource Management.* (pp. 615–629) Cambridge, MA: Blackwell.

Dalton, R. (1987). *Lifeplanning. A practical step-by-step guide to preparing for the happiest healthiest and wealthiest days of your life.* Scottsdale, AZ: Lifeplanning.

Danish, S., Smyer, M., et al. (1980). Developmental intervention: enhancing life-event processes. In P. Baltes & J. Brim (Eds.) *Life-Span Development and Behavior.* (pp. 339–366). Orville, NY: Academic Press.

Davey, L. (1991). The application of case study evaluations. *Practical Assessment, Research and Evaluation 2*(9).

Davies, H. (1997). Scaling the age barrier. *People Management 3,* 25–26.

Dennis, H., & Migliaccio J. (1997). Redefining retirement: The baby boomer challenge. *Generations, 21*(2), 45–50.

DeWitt, L. (1999). *The history and development of the social security retirement earnings test.* Washington, D.C: Social Security Administration.

Dexter, L. A. (1970). *Elite and specialized interviewing.* Evanston, IL: Northwestern University Press.

Dreher, G., & Kendall D. (1995). Organizational staffing. In G. Ferris, S. Rosen and D. Barnum (Eds.). *Handbook of Human Resource Management.* (pp. 446–461) Cambridge, MA: Blackwell.

Drucker, P. (1999) *Management challenges for the 21ˢᵗ century.* New York: Harper Business.

Drucker, P. (2001). The next society. *The Economist, 3*–5.

Dulebohn, J., Ferris, G., et al. (1995). History and evolution of human resource management. In G. Ferris, S. Rosen, & D. Barnum (Eds.), *Handbook of Human Resource Management.* (pp. 18–41) Cambridge, MA: Blackwell.

Dychtwald, K. (1999). *Age power: How the 21st century will be ruled by the new old.* New York: Penguin Putnam, Inc.

Eisen, M. (1998). Current practice and innovation in older adult learning. *New Directions for Adult and Continuing Education,* 77, 41–53.

Ekerdt, D. J., & Clark E. (2001). Selling retirement in financial planning advertisements. *Journal of Aging Studies, 15*(1), 55–68.

Ekerdt, D. J., & DeViney S. (1993). Evidence for a preretirement process among older male workers. *Journal of Gerontology, 48*(2), s35–s43.

Ekerdt, D. J., DeViney S., et al. (1996). Profiling plans for retirement. *Journal of Gerontology, 51*(Bn3).

Elder, G. H. J. (1992). The life course. *The Encyclopedia of Sociology.* E. F. Borgatta and M. L. Borgatta. New York: MacMillian.

Ellig, B., & Minehan M. (1998). *Future focus: HR in the 21st century.* Alexandria, VA: Society for Human Resource Management.

Erikson, E. (1963). *Childhood and society.* New York: Norton.

Erikson, E. (1974). *Dimensions of a new identity.* New York: W. W. Norton and Company, Inc.

Erikson, E. (1982). *The life cycle complete.* New York: W. W. Norton and Company.

Erikson, E., Erickson, J., et al. (1986). *Vital involvement in old age.* New York: W. W. Norton and Company.

Feldman, D. (1994). The decision to retire early: A review and conceptualization. *Academy of Management Review, 19*(2), 285–312.

Ferris, G., Barnum, D., et al. (1995). Toward business-university partnerships in human resource management: Integration of science and practice. In G. Ferris, S. Rosen, & D. Barnum (Eds). *Handbook of Human Resource Management.* (pp. 1–16) Cambridge, MA: Blackwell.

Ferris, G., Rosen, S., et al. (1995). *Handbook of human resource management.* Cambridge, MA: Blackwell.

Fowler, J. (1981). *Stages of faith: The psychology of human development and the quest for meaning.* New York: Harper San Francisco.

Frankl, V. (1992) *Man's search for meaning: an introduction to logotheraphy.* Boston: Beacon Press. (Original work published 1962)

Frey, L., Botan, C., et al. (1991). *Investigating communication. An introduction to research methods.* Englewood Cliffs, NJ: Prentice Hall.

Fronstin, P. (1999). Retirement patterns and employee benefits: Do benefits matter? *Gerontologist, 39*(1), 37–47.

Gall, T. L., & Evans, D. R. (2000). Preretirement expectations and the quality of life of male retirees in later retirement. *Canadian Journal of Behavioural Science 32*(3): 187–197.

Gardyn, R. (2000). Retirement redefined. *American Demographics, 22*(11), 51–57.

Gee, S., & Ballie, J. (1999). Happily ever after? An exploration of retirement expectations. *Educational Gerontology, 25,* 109–128.

Gendell, M. (2001). Retirement age declines again in 1990's. *Monthly Labor Review, 10,* 12–21.

Gerbman, R. (1999). Reach out with retirees: companies and their retirees extend their reach by partnering for volunteer work. *HR Magazine, 44*(2), 74–78.

Gowan, M. (1998). A preliminary investigation of factors affecting appraisal of the decision to take early retirement. *Journal of Employment Counseling, 35*(3), 124–141.

Hall, J. (1999). Staying current on laws is key to plan success. *Workforce, 78* (9), 84–85.

Hayes, C., & Parker, M. (1993). Overview of the literature on preretirement planning for women. *Journal of Women and Aging, 4*(4), 1–18.

Henkens, K. (1999). Retirement intentions and spousal support: A multi-actor approach. *Journal of Gerontology, 54*(Bn2).

Hettler, B. (1980). Wellness promotion on a university campus. *Family and Community Health, 3*(1), 77–95.

Hummer, R. (1999). Religious involvement and U.S. Adult mortality. *Demography,* 36(2), 273–285.

Hunter, W. (1980) *Preretirement education leader's manual.* Ann Arbor, MI: The University of Michigan.

Hurd, M., & McGarry, K. (1995). Evaluation of the subjective probabilities of survival in the health and retirement study. *The Journal of Human Resources,* 30, s268–s292.

Ivancevich, J. (1998). *Human Resource Management.* Boston: McGraw Hill.

Kahn, R., & Antonucci, T. (1980). Convoys over the life course: attachment, roles, and social support. In P. Baltes & J. Brim (Eds.) *Life-Span Development and Behavior.* (pp. 254–286) Orville, NY: Academic Press. *3,* 254–286.

Kazel, Robert. Retirement education takes multiple approaches. *Business Insurance,* 33(19), p. 3–4.

Kiefer, T., & Briner, R. (1998). Managing retirement—Rethinking links between individual and organization. *European Journal of Work and Organizational Psychology,* 7(3), 373–390.

Kim, S., & Feldman, D.(2000). Working in Retirement: the antecedents of bridge employment and its consequences for quality of life in retirement. *Academy of Management Journal, 43*(6), 1195–1210.

Kubler-Ross, E. (1969). *On death and dying.* New York: Macmillian.

Kvale, S. (1996). *InterViews: An introduction to qualitative research interviewing.* Thousand Oaks, CA: Sage.

Lach, J. (1999). Dateline America: May 1, 2025. *American Demographics, 21*(5), 19–21.

Lassey, W., & Lassey, M. (2001). *Quality of life for older people: An international perspective.* Upper Saddle River: Prentice Hall.

Leder, D. (2000). Aging into the spirit: from traditional wisdom to innovative programs and communities. *Generations, 23*(4), 36–42.

Lee, C. (1996). *Essays on retirement and wealth accumulation in the United States, 1850–1990.* Chicago, IL: University of Chicago.

LeRoy, M., & Schultz, J. (1995). The legal context of human resource management: Conflict, confusion, cost and role conversion. In G. Ferris, S. Rosen, & D. Barnum (Eds.), *Handbook of Human Resource Management* (pp. 143–158).Cambridge, MA: Blackwell.

Lincoln, Y. S., & Guba, E. G. (1985). *Naturalistic inquiry.* Beverly Hills, CA: Sage Publications.

Lindahl, L. (1949). What makes a good job? *Personnel*, 25, 262–266.

Lindbo, T., & Schultz, K. (1998). The role of organizational culture and mentoring in mature worker socialization toward retirement. *Public Productivity & Management Review*, 22(1), 49–59.

Lo, R., & Brown, R. (1999). Stress and adaptation: Preparation for successful retirement. *Austrailian and New Zealand Journal of Mental Health Nursing*, 8, 30–38.

Lofland, J., & Loftland, L. (1995). *Analyzing social settings: A guide to qualitative observation and analysis*. Belmont, CA: Wadsworth.

Marshall, V. W., Clark, P. J., et al. (2001). Instability in the retirement transition: Effects on health and well-being in a Canadian study. *Research on Aging*, 23(4), 379–420.

Maslow, A. (1971). *The farther reaches of human nature*. New York: Viking Press.

Maule, A. J. (1995). Early retirement schemes: Factors governing their success and how these differ across job categories. *Personnel Review*, 24(8), 6–16.

Mergerhagen, P. (1994). Rethinking retirement. *American Demographics*, 16(6), 28–33.

Merriam, S. B. (1988). *Case study research in education*. San Francisco: Jossey-Bass.

Merton, R. K. (1957). *Social theory and social structure*. Glencoe, IL: Free Press.

Mindell, A. (1995). *Sitting in the fire. Large group transformation using conflict and diversity*. Portland, OR: Lao Tse Press.

Moen, P. (1998). Recasting careers: changing reference groups, risks and realities. *Generations*, 22(1), 40–45.

Moen, P., Dempster-McClain, D. et al. (1989). Social integration and longevity: An event history analysis of women's roles and resilience. *American Sociological Review*, 54, 635–647.

Moore, K., & Biordi, D. (1995). Nurses' retirement preparation. *Journal of Nursing Preparation, 25*, 62–67.

Murrell, S., Norris, F. H., et al. (1988). Life events in older adults. In L.H. Cohen (Eds.), *Life Events and Psychological Functioning and Methodological Issues.* (pp. 96–122) Beverly Hills, CA: Sage Publications.

n.a. (1987). *Webster's compact dictionary.* Springfield, MA: Merriam-Webster.

n.a. (2003) *Employee retirement income security act—ERISA.* Department of Labor. Retrieved on July 8, 2003 from http://www.dol.gov/dol/topic/health-plans/erisa.htm.

n.a. (2003) *Employee benefits law.* Illinois Employee Benefits Law. Retrieved on July 8, 2003 from http://www.weblocator.com/attorney/il/law/empben.html.

n.a. (2001). Few employers have a plan to manage baby boomers nearing retirement. *HR Focus, 4*(Apr 2001), 8–9.

n.a. (2002). *Institute for learning in retirement,* Northwestern University. *2002.*

n.a. (2001) *Senior corps.* Corporation for National Service. Retrieved on February 2, 2003 from http://www.nationalservice.org/.

n.a. (2003) *Your special blend.* Starbucks. Retrieved on July 2, 2003 from http://www.starbucks.com/aboutus/SB-YSB-US-HR.pdf.

Northwestern University. (2002) *Institute for learning in retirement.* Northwestern University. Retrieved on February 2, 2003 from http://www.scs.northwestern.edu/nuilr/.

Oman, D., Thorsesen, C., et al. (1999). Volunteerism and mortality among the community-dwelling elderly. *Journal of Health Psychology,* 4(3), 301–316.

Peck, M. S. (1993). *Further along the road less traveled.* New York: Simon & Schuster.

Peck, M. S. (1994). *A world waiting to be born.* New York: Bantam Books.

Pillermer, K., Moen, P., et al. (1995). Setting the White House conference on aging agenda: recommendations from an expert panel. *Gerontologist, 35(2)*, 258–261.

Poulos, S. (1997). *The aging baby boom: Implications for employment and training programs*. Washington, D.C., United States Department of Labor.

Purcell, P. (2000). Older workers: Employment and retirement trends. *Monthly Labor Review, 123*(10), 19–30.

Quick, H. E., & Moen, P., (1998). Gender, employment, and retirement quality: A life course approach to differential experiences of men and women. *Journal of Occupational Health Psychology, 3*(1), 44–64.

Raphael, T. (2002). Let's teach employees to retire. *Workforce, 81*(2), 80.

Riley, M. W., & Riley, Jr., J. W. (1994). Structual lag: Past and future. In M.W. Reily, R. L. Kahn, & A. Foner (Eds.), *Age and Structural Lag: The mismatch between people's lives and opportunities in work, family and leisure,* (pp. 15–36). New York:Wiley.

Rosenkoetter, M. M., & Garris, J. M. (2001). Retirement planning, use of time, and psychological adjustment. *Issues in Mental Health Nursing, 22,* 703–722.

Rosenkoetter, M. M., Garris, J. M., et al. (2001). Postretirement use of time: Implications for preretirement planning and postretirement management. *Activities, Adaptation & Aging, 25*(3–4), 1–18.

Sandelowski, M. (1995) Rigo or rigor mortis: The problem of rigor in qualitative research revisited. *Advances in Nursing Science, 16* (2), 1–8.

Samuelson, R. (1999). Off golden pond. *The New Republic, 220*(15), 36–38.

Schieber, S. (1996). The sleeping giant awakens: U. S. retirement policy in the 21st century. *Compensation and Benefits Review, 28,* 20–31.

Schweiger, D., Gosselin, A., et al. (1995). Preserving and realizing acquisition value through human resources practices. In G. Ferris, S. Rosen, & D. Barnum (Eds.), *Handbook of Human Resources*. Cambridge, MA: Blackwell.

Sheehy, G. (1995). *New passages: Mapping your life across time.* New York: Ballatine Books.

Smith, B. (1994). Retiree programs link skills with needs. *HR Focus,* 71(10), 7.

Smith, D., & Moen, P. (1998). Spousal influence on retirement: His, her, and their perceptions. *Journal of Marriage and the Family, 60*(3), 734–744.

Smith, M. (2001). The military retirement reform act of 1986 or Redux: a postmortem. *Journal of Political and Military Sociology, 29*(Winter), 305–318.

Smith, W. (2001). *Hope Meadows: real life stories of healing and caring from an inspired community.* New York: Penguin Putnam Inc.

SSA (2002a.). *Detailed chronology,* Social Security Adminstration.

SSA (2002b). *Social security reform,* Social Security Administration.

SSA, (2002c). *Age 65 retirement,* Social Security Administration.

Stake, R. (1991). Case studies. In N. Denzin & Y. Lincoln (Eds.), *Handbook of Qualitative Research.* Thousand Oaks, CA: Sage Publications.

Stein, D. (2000). *The new meaning of retirement.* Columbus, OH: Office of Educational Research and Improvement.

Steinbrink, J. E. & Cook, J. W. (2002). Understanding social security: A civic obligation. *Social Studies, 93*(5), 209–213.

Sullivan, S. (1992). Effects of career stage on retirement: A longitudinal analysis. *International Journal of Career Management,* 4(1), 7–16.

Sunoo, B. (1997). Millions may retire. *Workforce, 76*(Dec. 1997), 48–50.

Swanson, E., & Kopecky, K. (1999). Lifespan and output. *Economic Inquiry, 37*(2), 213–225.

Talaga, J. A., &. Beehr, T. A.(1995). Are there gender differences in predicting retirement decisions? *Journal of Applied Psychology, 80*(1), 0021–9010.

Tellis, W. (1997). Introduction to case study. *The Qualitative Report,* 3(2), 1–12.

Thompson, R. (1999). What, me worry? *HR Magazine, 44*(11), 62–72.

Tizard, B., & Owen, C. (2001). Activities and attitudes of retired university staff. *Oxford Review of Education, 27(2)*.

Tribe, C. (1982). *Profile of three theories Erikson Maslow Piaget.* Dubuque, IA: Kendall/Hunt Publishing Company.

Vidich, A., & Lyman, S. (2000). Qualitative methods. Their history in sociology and anthropology. In N. Denzin & Y. Lincoln (Eds.), *Handbook of Qualitative Research* (pp. 37–84). Thousand Oaks, CA: Sage Publications.

Wagner, C. (1999). The centenarians are coming! *Futurist, 33*(5), 16–18.

Walker, J. (1996). Concepts of retirement in historical perspective. In J. Walker (Eds.), *Changing Concepts of Retirement,* (pp. 3–21). Brookfield, VT: Ashgate Publishing Company.

Ward, S. (1999). Making sense of Social Security reform. *Workforce, 78(*10), 76–82.

Wellner, A. S. (1999). Workplace 2018: retirement boom or bust? *Training, 36*(8), 54–59.

Williamson, J. B. (2002). What's next for Social Security? Partial privatization? *Generations, 26*(2), 34–40.

Yin, R. K. (1989). *Case study research: Design and methods.* Newbury Park, CA: Sage.

Yin, R. K. (1993). *Applications of case study research.* Thousand Oaks, CA: Sage Publications.

Yin, R. K. (1994). *Case study research: design and methods.* Thousand Oaks, CA: SAGE Publications.

APPENDIX

Interview Schedule

Question 1: Financial Planning

---

a. What type of financial planning information for retirement did you receive from your organization?

b. Were you satisfied with the training?

c. What information was relevant to your current experience in retirement?

Question 2: Estate Planning

---

a. What type of estate planning information for retirement did you receive from your organization?

b. Were you satisfied with the training?

c. What information was relevant to your current experience in retirement?

Question 3: Will Preparation

---

a. What type of will preparation information for retirement did you receive from your organization?

b. Were you satisfied with the training?

c. What information was relevant to your current experience in retirement?

Question 4: Power of Attorney

---

a. What type of Power of Attorney information for retirement did you receive from your organization?

b. Were you satisfied with the training?

c. What information was relevant to your current experience in retirement?

Question 5: Eldercare Planning

---

a. What type of eldercare planning information for retirement did you receive from your organization?

b. Were you satisfied with the training?

c. What information was relevant to your current experience in retirement?

Question 6: Resume Writing

a.   What type of resume writing information for retirement did you receive from your organization?

b.   Were you satisfied with the training?

c.   What information was relevant to your current experience in retirement?

Question 7: Health Benefits

a.   What type of health benefit planning information for retirement did you receive from your organization?

b.   Were you satisfied with the training?

c.   What information was relevant to your current experience in retirement?

Question 8: Technology and Computer Usage

a.   What type of technology and computer usage information for retirement did you receive from your organization?

b.   Were you satisfied with the training?

c.   What information was relevant to your current experience in retirement?

Question 9: Career Coaching

a.   What type of career coaching information for retirement did you receive from your organization?

b.   Were you satisfied with the training?

c.   What information was relevant to your current experience in retirement?

Question 10: Other Questions

a.   What other training or preparation was offered by your organization before you retired?

b.   What other training or preparation did you participate in to prepare to retire?

Question 11: Wealth

a.   What type of financial planning, if any, did you conduct in preparation for retirement?

b.   What, if anything, would you change about your financial planning for retirement?

Question 12: Geography

    a.   What type of geographical planning, if any, did you conduct in preparation for retirement?

    b.   What, if anything, would you change about your geographical planning for retirement?

Question 13: Companionship

    a.   What type of companionship planning, if any, did you conduct in preparation for retirement?

    b.   What, if anything, would you change about your companionship planning for retirement?

Question 14: Physical Fitness

    a.   What type of physical fitness planning, if any, did you conduct in preparation for retirement?

    b.   What, if anything, would you change about your physical fitness planning for retirement?

Question 15: Physical Nutrition

    a.   What type of physical nutrition planning, if any, did you conduct in preparation for retirement?

    b.   What, if anything, would you change about your physical nutrition for retirement?

Question 16: Emotional Awareness

    a.   What type of emotional awareness planning, if any, did you conduct in preparation for retirement?

    b.   What, if anything, would you change about your emotional awareness planning for retirement?

Question 17: Emotional Control

    a.   What type of emotional control planning, if any, did you conduct in preparation for retirement?

    b.   What, if anything, would you change about your emotional control planning for retirement?

Question 18: Intellectual

    a.   What type of intellectual planning, if any, did you conduct in preparation for retirement?

    b.   What, if anything, would you change about your intellectual planning for retirement?

Question 19: Occupational

    a.   What type of occupational planning, if any, did you conduct in preparation for retirement?

    b.   What, if anything, would you change about your occupational planning for retirement?

Question 20: Spiritual

    a.   What type of spiritual planning, if any, did you conduct in preparation for retirement?

    b.   What, if anything, would you change about your spiritual planning for retirement?

Question 21: Planning for Retirement

    a.   What led you to select the age you retired?

    b.   When did you decide to retire early?

    c.   What factors did you consider about your decision to retire early?

    d.   What decisions and choices did you make about early retirement? (use of time, etc.)

    e.   What did you think was the ideal type retirement before you retired?

    f.   Are you doing what you thought you would in retirement?

    g.   What are you doing in your retirement?

    h.   Have you worked for pay since you retired? What have you done?

    i.   Have you started a new career or entered a new field? If so, what?

    j.   Are there areas of freedom or fear related to your retirement?

    k.   What do you miss, if anything, since you retired?

    l.   If you were to coach someone preparing to retire, what would you tell them?

    m.   Is there anything else you would like to say about your retirement?

About the Author

Dr. Maria K. Malayter

Dr. Malayter has a dynamic and diverse 15+ year career as a highly rated trainer, college professor, marketing specialist, negotiator, and consultant for public and private organizations across the country. Her scope of experience includes: leadership training, project management, instructional technology, e-learning, concept sales, human resources management, operations management, public relations, instructional design, organizational development, management consulting and educational planning. Dr. Malayter has delivered substantial revenue and productivity gains in new markets and returned multimillion dollar projects to profitability.

Dr. Malayter attended Ball State University for her bachelor and master degree and completed her doctoral studies in Leadership and Organizational Change at Walden University. Dr. Malayter has been a college professor of Applied Behavioral Science at National-Louis University and currently is the

Assistant Dean of the College of Arts and Science at NLU. She previously has taught for Ball State University, College of DuPage, Valencia Community College, Brevard Community College, Rollins College, College of Lake County and Webster University. Committed to mentoring, she continues to volunteer for Alpha Sigma Alpha national sorority and Junior Achievement of Chicago. Dr. Malayter is an enthusiastic, positive, and results driven individual with strong training, communication and leadership skills.

Dr. Maria Malayter's signature consulting areas include:
Communication and Personal Development Seminars
Distance Learning and Training Consulting and Seminars
Retirement Transition Seminars

Please visit her company website, Innovations in Change at docmaria.com.

0-595-31506-2